MORE PRAISE

"Those doctors who attend to the interpersonal side of medicine will appreciate this book, and 'mechanical' doctors will ignore it. Perhaps it could be assigned to those guys."

—Richard Mark Steinbook, MD
Emeritus Professor of Psychiatry and Behavioral Science
University of Miami

"During medical school, we were dazzled by Bob's magical performances as we watched him becoming a first-rate physician. With this book, he applies both of these talents to show other doctors how to cope with the many challenges of contemporary medical practice. This book is a fascinating performance by a truly inspired physician."

—Jack M. Gorman, MD
CEO and Chief Scientific Officer at Franklin Behavioral Consultants

"Why don't they teach these strategies in medical school and nursing school?! Baker offers a novel approach to delivering a patient experience that can immediately improve patient outcomes and satisfaction."

—Shep Hyken
Customer Service Expert
New York Times bestselling author of *The Amazement Revolution*

"I plan to order copies as holiday gifts for my work partners."

—Raj Madhok, MD
Dermatology Specialists, Edina, MN

ALSO BY BOB BAKER, MD

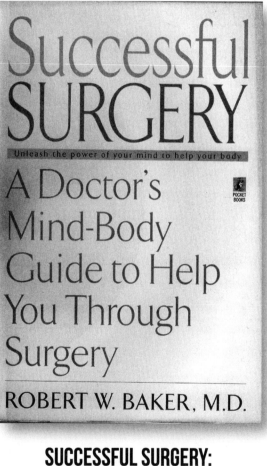

SUCCESSFUL SURGERY:
A DOCTOR'S MIND-BODY GUIDE
TO HELP YOU THROUGH SURGERY

BOB BAKER, MD

THE PERFORMANCE OF MEDICINE:

TECHNIQUES FROM THE STAGE TO OPTIMIZE THE PATIENT EXPERIENCE AND RESTORE THE JOY OF PRACTICING MEDICINE

BEST JOB PRODUCTIONS, LLC

For my patients.
For the healers.

And for Marcia.

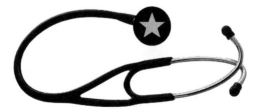

CONTENTS

Foreword...*xi*

Introduction..*1*

SECTION I
WHERE WE ARE

Chapter 1: The Changing Medical World............................*15*

Chapter 2: The Patient Visit Is a Performance....................*28*

Chapter 3: I'm Not a Performer and Don't Want to Be........*39*

Chapter 4: What Patients Want *48*

SECTION II
TECHNIQUES AND STRATEGIES

Chapter 5: The Five Basic Performance Techniques We Need........*63*

Chapter 6: Setting the Stage *78*

Chapter 7: In the Room with the Patient............................*92*

Chapter 8: The Performance Must Go On *111*

Chapter 9: Improvisation and Storytelling..........................*124*

SECTION III
MOVING AHEAD

Chapter 10: Putting It All to Work......................................*139*

Chapter 11: When Things Go Wrong...................................*145*

Chapter 12: What Others Say..*154*

Chapter 13: Curtain..*164*

APPENDICES

Collected Takeaways *169*

Appendix I: Dr. Adam Smith's Script *177*

Appendix II: Charles "Buck" Adams on Body Language *181*

Appendix III: Norman Kanter, PhD on Handling Anger *187*

Appendix IV: What Really Happened at America's Got Talent *195*

Acknowledgments *199*

References *205*

Author's Note: Although I wrote this book for physicians, it applies equally to all other direct healthcare providers: nurses, nurse practitioners, physician's assistants, chiropractors, physical therapists, and even dentists. If you are any of these, please substitute yourself whenever I refer to doctors.

FOREWORD

In April 2016 I had the privilege of arranging a presentation on patient experience by my friend Dr. Bob Baker for colleagues at my hospital. Before the date, we discussed how his presentation, titled *The Performance of Medicine: Putting the Patient Experience Center Stage* would explain how he uses his experience as a magician and ventriloquist to attain super patient satisfaction. I admit I was more than skeptical. I did not see how making a dummy talk or how smoke and mirrors could improve our Press Ganey scores. However, with his survey ratings ranking him consistently at the 99th percentile nationally, I knew he must be onto something, or he was practicing real hocus-pocus. Either way, I was interested and more than impressed at the end of his presentation when those in attendance said they were eager to put into practice the simple strategies he taught: techniques used by all performers to delight their audiences and which Dr. Baker uses to connect with his patients.

For thirty-five years, Dr. Bob Baker has been a practicing gastro-enterologist in a competitive and demanding market where patient expectations go well past preventing and healing illness, and care experiences are judged equally on the quality of the interactions between caregivers and their patients. Dr. Baker has consistently received the highest ratings possible by his patients in reviews and on patient surveys. He has thrived in the modern healthcare paradigm using the performance skills he's borrowed from an even longer career onstage, skills he explains in this book.

Dr. Baker sets the stage by jocularly tracing his journey through the business of healthcare, which has changed dramatically since his days as a medical student. He starts before insurers became involved in medical decisions and doctor reimbursement and continues through today, when the pressure is greater than ever to do more with less. In this new environment, doctors need to understand what patients want, need, and expect. Physicians must use skills they may not have learned in medical school to make every moment with the patient magical. No longer is it acceptable to deliver healthcare while focusing only on diagnosis and treatment, and with service pushed backstage and out of sight. Today, the entire patient experience is subject to review.

Dr. Baker approaches every patient interaction as a performance and shows, in this book, how doctors can incorporate the techniques used by every performer before, during, and after patient interactions to turn each encounter into a five-star patient experience. Dr. Baker borrows from his long career in front of large audiences to delight the small audiences in his exam room. His techniques are based on sound research in the field of service excellence by some of the most prominent experts on the topic of patient experience as well as from the accumulated knowledge of award-winning thespians.

I know you what you're thinking. You're not an actor. Well, rest assured, you don't have to enroll in The Juilliard School to become a better doctor or nurse. There's an actor in all of us, and you already have many of the skills needed to perform better in the exam room. You just need to use them, and Dr. Baker explains how, when, and, more importantly, why to use them in a straightforward manner that is easy to understand. With the essential points highlighted at the end of each chapter, this book makes it effortless to retain its central ideas, much the same way a competent practitioner discharges his patients with a concise list of the signs and symptoms to look out for. Dr. Baker shares plenty of anecdotes that will make you laugh as you read them, but the concepts presented are based on science, years of his personal experience, and plenty of trial and error.

The Performance of Medicine is primarily intended for doctors in outpatient practices, but the information and techniques work for nurses, nurse practitioners, technicians, and in hospitals as well as in outpatient settings.

As a hospital administrator who has worked most of my professional life trying to improve patient satisfaction, I wish every doctor with privileges in my hospital would read this book and put Dr. Baker's techniques to work. They are easy to implement. They will not add more time to encounters, but they work like magic and will make every patient experience worthy of a standing ovation.

—Michael Maione
Director of Customer Relations
Stony Brook University Hospital

INTRODUCTION

We've all been patients too.

I was in my urologist's office, sitting on a small exam table where I was about to undergo an outpatient vasectomy[*]. Yes, I was a bit anxious. The visit up until then had gone smoothly enough. The receptionist was efficient, if not overly friendly, and a pleasant medical assistant had escorted me to the small procedure room and told me to remove all my clothes except underwear.

The minutes ticked by. This was years before I had a smartphone to distract myself. There were no magazines, even old, tattered ones, to look at. I had surveyed the contents of the room several times already. I had refreshed my knowledge of my personal anatomy from the anatomical chart hanging on the wall and was hoping it was not there for my doctor to refer to. Now there was nothing to do but sit and wait. And wait.

Finally, the door opened, and there stood the most severe-looking nurse I had ever seen. She wore a starched white uniform, and her steel-gray hair was pulled back in a bun tight enough to give her a rhytidoplasty.

She stood in the doorway for a few endless seconds and, in an accent reminiscent of Frau Blücher[†] from *Young Frankenstein*, hissed these exact words: "Take off your T-shirt. You're going to *sweat* a little." And walked out.

I nearly passed out.

However, ten years before that I had quite a different patient experience. On a Friday morning in 1981, Boston obstetrician Dr.

---

[*] Let's get personal right off the bat, shall we?

[†] https://www.youtube.com/watch?v=hs5j8uUR2nc

Kenneth Blotner ruptured my wife's membranes to induce labor for our overdue first child. It was Dr. Blotner's weekend to be off, but he agreed to induce "us," I guess because he recognized that the Bakers were a little bit anxious about childbirth and had only seen the covering doctor once.

So Dr. Blotner did the deed, started a Pitocin drip, and we waited. And waited. The labor progressed slowly. Twenty-one hours worth of slowly.

I recall very little of those twenty-one hours except being scolded once during Lamaze coaching/breathing for having "Frito breath."

One thing I will never forget, though, is that Dr. Blotner assured us, without our asking, that he—and not the covering doc—would be present to deliver our baby no matter when he arrived that weekend— which he did at 1:21 Saturday morning.

We moved away from Boston, and I'm sure Dr. Blotner forgot us among the many acts of kindness he performed in his lifetime. But we never forgot him.

All of us practitioners have stories, good and bad, about our experiences with other health professionals, be they doctors, nurses, nurse practitioners, physician's assistants, etc. The stories might be entertaining, instructive, harrowing, or all three, but they've just been stories. They didn't count for anything. Until now.

Today, patients report their experiences and rate us in surveys from health systems, insurance companies, and the government. They can post reviews about us online and grade us like hotels, restaurants, roofers, and plumbers*. Less than stellar ratings can lower our income, prevent us from attracting new patients, and even get us kicked off an insurance company's panel of providers. We *must* provide patients with excellent experiences.

That's why this book is necessary now. Our ratings and patient satisfaction scores are going to play a big role in our futures. If we're

---

* Actually, as a gastroenterologist, I don't resent being rated like a plumber. We sort of do the same thing. They just get paid more.

not getting top scores, we'd better perform better. *If* we perform better, there are the added benefits that our patients' outcomes will improve *and* we will enjoy practicing more—or again.

So: a book called *The Performance of Medicine*. Long ago I came to the realization that when any health practitioner interacts with a patient, it's a performance. Not a show, but a performance.* And by bringing into the exam room the skills that a performer uses to connect with and win over an audience, we can improve the experience for our patients and ourselves. We just have to learn how.

Keep in mind from the outset that the goal of any performance is to *connect with* and *communicate with* the audience. This is true whether the performance is Bruce Springsteen playing a concert for twenty thousand people or you telling a joke to a friend. And it's true when you are in the exam room or at the bedside with a patient. He or she is your audience. It is only through connecting with the patient that the magic of medicine can begin.

★   ★   ★

IN OUR NEW WORLD, WHICH I'll discuss in detail in Chapter 1, the fact that we are good doctors with good results is no longer enough. As physicians, we've been trained to concentrate on outcomes. Does the patient get better? Live longer? Does he live at all? For the last century, those results have been pretty much what mattered to us. Yes, the humanist element of medicine has always been important, but now the concepts of "patient satisfaction" and "patient experience" are gaining prominence, and we ignore them at our own risk.

The risk is to our reputations, our practices, and our incomes. What patients think about us and what they experience in our offices and hospitals is now public information, freely available to anyone with

---

* It was Dr. Ricardo Rosenkranz of Northwestern University's Feinberg School of Medicine who enunciated that distinction.

Internet access and fingers. Actually, fingers are optional. And it doesn't even matter if what patients report is true.

A few years ago, an elderly woman made an appointment to see one of my partners as a new patient. On the day of her visit, coming up to the office in the elevator, she suffered a cardiac arrest. The people in the building called us to help, so we grabbed our crash cart and ran to the elevator. We worked on her until the ambulance arrived, but to no avail. She passed away. She never even made it into the office for her first appointment.

However, the story that went around town and found its way onto social media was that she had arrested on the way *down* in the elevator, *after* seeing my partner. Unfortunately, that's the kind of story people like to tell.

In this era when information and *mis*information are freely available to all, it's more important than ever that health practitioners strive to give patients the best possible experience. But what does that mean? What do patients want? How do we give it to them and make sure they *know* we're giving it to them?

You'll find the answers in this book.

There are certainly other books about the patient experience, and I'll point you to some of those in Chapter 12, What Others Say. The big difference between some of those books and this one is that I'm not trying to make you a better, more compassionate, more empathic doctor, nurse, or other health practitioner. You already are sufficiently compassionate and empathic. Instead, I'm giving you tools—techniques and strategies—that you can add to your already considerable medical and humanistic skills to give your patients an even better experience than they now get from you.

Think of it this way: Even the greatest athletes in the world still have coaches and trainers to help them stay at the tops of their games. The most successful CEOs have business and leadership coaches to help them in the running of their companies. Even Supreme Court justices have clerks to assist them in staying abreast of relevant laws.

Every one of these people needs to perform at his or her best every single day, and they recognize the need for help to maximize their performances.

Performances. They're all around us every day. We perform many roles ourselves—doctor, spouse, parent—even if we don't realize it. In Chapter 2, we'll examine how we are all performing all the time. If you don't agree with me, let me, for now, leave you with the words of the Bard: "All the world's a stage, And all the men and women merely players... And one man in his time plays many parts."[1] Go argue with him.

If we bring techniques from the stage into the practice of medicine, we can create a better experience for our patients. And who can better show us how to do that than a seasoned performer?

With all modesty, that brings us to me. Sure, for nearly thirty-five years I was an internist and gastroenterologist in one of the busiest multi-specialty internal medicine practices on the North Shore of Long Island; but for fifty years I've been a professional magician and ventriloquist. Guess which I'm prouder of. Actually, that's being a doctor, though the other hasn't hurt—and even helped get me into medical school. Really.

When I interviewed for admission to Columbia University's College of Physicians and Surgeons, the interviewer, the eminent Dr. Andrew G. Frantz[*], looked at my application and said, "You say here you're a magician. Do something for me." I was quite taken aback. I'd never been asked to perform at an interview and certainly hadn't prepared anything.

Fortunately, I had a single playing card in my wallet to use for emergencies. A playing card in the wallet is, for magicians, like a condom in the wallet for a teenage boy: You sort of know you're never going to need it, but it's nice to know it's there. I pried the card out of my wallet and made it disappear and then reappear at my fingertips. Dr. Frantz laughed and clapped his hands. "Show me more."

---

[*] He was the first to isolate prolactin.

So I borrowed some quarters from him and made them travel invisibly from hand to hand. He loved it. We concluded the interview on a happy note, and a few weeks later I received my acceptance letter to P&S.

The confluence of magician and physician goes all the way back to their respective origins. Consider this: We know what the oldest profession is, but what's the second oldest? Hunter-gatherer? Nah, everybody did that, so it isn't a profession. Primitive politician? That's a tautology. Neolithic attorney? Nope. Just a variant on the oldest profession.

I strongly suspect that the second oldest profession was healer/ magician. Fire up Mr. Peabody's Wayback* time machine and you'll probably find that the first healers were regarded as magicians and vice versa.

So I'm not ashamed to admit that I'm both a physician and a magician, though I usually tried to keep them separate. I was a magician long before I was a physician, and medicine and magic have intertwined themselves throughout my life. And magic has taken me places I never thought I'd go. For instance, to a command performance for tribal elders at a Bedouin wedding in the Negev desert.

A radiologist gave me my first book on magic. For my bar mitzvah, Dr. Myron Melamed and his family gave me *Successful Conjuring for Amateurs* by Norman Hunter. The Melameds knew I had already taught myself ventriloquism and that I had an insatiable curiosity about how things worked, so a book on magic was a natural.

I've read that book more times than I've read *Green Eggs and Ham*, and I have seven kids. *Successful Conjuring* was one so-that's-how-they-do-it revelation after another. I started performing tricks from the book for anyone who would watch—my younger siblings, my parents. The former were an eager audience; the latter were tolerant, mostly.

---

*WABAC, for Peabody purists: http://www.toonopedia.com/peabody.htm

The next great influence was our family pediatrician in New Jersey, Dr. Louis Krafchik. He sweetened visits for childhood vaccinations with magic tricks—some fairly sophisticated, as I look back on his performances. I remember thinking, "A doctor who does magic. That's cool!"

As my own interest in medicine and my magic skills grew, I decided I wanted to be a pediatrician, mostly so that I could perform magic for my young patients the way Dr. Krafchik did. Even performing at kids' birthday parties through high school did not dampen this desire. However, taking care of fatally ill children during my pediatrics rotations in medical school did. Hence, I became an internist for adults.

Performing magic, ventriloquism, and hypnosis stood me in good stead in the lean financial years of medical school. I arranged my elective schedule so I'd have easy summers, allowing me to perform in the Catskill Mountains' famous "Borscht Belt" on weekends.

You've paid your performing dues when you start a show at one o'clock in the morning for an audience that has just returned from a losing night at nearby Monticello Raceway. Or when you introduce yourself to the entertainment director, who says, "Hypnotist?? We were told we were having a stripper!" I did my hypnosis show fully clothed anyway.

I continued to perform magic and mentalism through my fellowship years and then for fundraisers and private events once I went into practice. I also performed ventriloquism for friends, family, and private groups I belonged to until 2008, when I asked myself if I was good enough to entertain people who didn't know me and wouldn't be rooting for me. I took a course in stand-up comedy at a local comedy club and began performing in clubs on Long Island and in New York City as well as at numerous private parties, fundraisers, and church and synagogue shows.

In 2013, my ventriloquism mentor, the legendary (among show people) Sammy King, suggested that I audition for the NBC television show *America's Got Talent*. I decided to perform with my talking large intestine puppet, Sigmoid Colon. Hey, I'm a gastroenterologist, okay?

However, before my audition for the "celebrity judges," I was informed that the producers had learned that one of the judges, Howard Stern, was my patient.* They told me they saw a conflict of interest and that, no matter how well I did, they were not going to let me advance to the next round.

That was okay. I had a good day job and I got to perform ventriloquism on TV in prime time for eleven million people. You can watch my audition on YouTube†, but know that the producers actually changed two of the judges' votes to assure that I would not progress to the next round. You can read what *really* happened on *AGT* in the somewhat self-indulgent Appendix IV.

Back to the patient experience and this book. I've strived to make the book practical, to the point, and, because I like entertaining people, enjoyable to read for the practitioner who already has too much to read and too little time to do it. To accomplish these goals, I've limited the book's scope and thrown in a few jokes.

"Patient experience" and "patient satisfaction" encompass a very big universe involving health systems, administrators, CEOs, employees, institutes, researchers, etc. Those terms incorporate what happens to patients in hospitals, what the government wants hospitals to do, how patient experience should be measured and reimbursed, and on and on. None of that macrocosm is the purview of this book. I have concentrated on the one aspect of the patient experience *we* can control—the precious few minutes we have in direct face-to-face contact with the patient.

Unlike some other books on the subject, my goal is not to make you a better doctor. I don't want to completely change how you communicate with patients, but rather to give you some simple tools to do so more

---

* No HIPAA violation here. He's told his twelve million listeners that I was his doctor, so I can tell you.

† https://www.youtube.com/watch?v=9nP7gpou9qs

effectively. I'll offer you some easily implemented techniques and strategies that will improve the patient experience and the ratings your patients give you.

Now, you might accuse me of "teaching to the test," of just suggesting superficial things to make patients happier and get you better ratings. Nothing—well, few things—could be further from the truth. You see, I already believe that you're a caring, empathic person. It's part of why you became a caregiver. So I want to give you practical ideas to supplement the strengths you already have, not ask you to develop new ones.

By putting these techniques and strategies into practice, not only will your patients have a better experience, but you will too. You'll enjoy practicing more. As we'll discuss in Chapter 2, a good performance benefits the audience *and* the performer.

My approach to the patient experience is one I've developed from nearly thirty-five years of private practice and fifty years of performing onstage and has garnered me excellent Press Ganey scores and online reviews. I'll offer many ideas from which you can choose those that appeal to you. They are all easily implemented without making huge changes in your staff, your practice, or yourself. And, very importantly, they don't take any more of your precious time.

★　★　★

IT TOOK ME ABOUT FORTY-FOUR years and ten months to write this book.

That's four years of medical school, three of internal medicine residency, two of GI fellowship and then almost thirty-five of medical practice. Those years comprise over a hundred thousand patient visits, every one of them unique. I also performed about twenty thousand endoscopic procedures, not so unique since a lot of stomachs and colons look pretty much the same. There were countless routine physicals, URIs, UTIs, irritable bowels and refluxing esophagi, serious and fatal illnesses, weird infections, stress-related illnesses, easy cases, head-scratchers, triumphant diagnoses, social issues, family tragedies, and three mistakes that haunt me to this day.

Then came the ten months of researching, writing, editing, and rewriting to actually get it all into a book. What I included I learned from my many years of practice, from a review of the literature, and also from interviewing superior physicians with excellent patient ratings. They let me pick their brains and ask them what specific things they did to satisfy their patients.

One such interview stands out in my memory. I talked with an experienced and much-beloved internist who is consistently one of the highest-rated physicians in our area. I asked, "What's your secret?"

"I give every patient a thirty-minute visit."

"Come again?"

"Yes, every routine appointment in my office is thirty minutes, except yearly physicals; they're an hour."

"Wait a minute," I interrupted. "What about routine blood pressure checks?"

"Thirty minutes."

"Viral URIs?"

"They get half an hour," he sort-of joked.

"Those things don't require thirty minutes to take care of. What do you do the rest of the time?"

"I schmooze with them."

If your practice runs that way, please put this book down and get your money back. I have nothing to teach you. But if you're harried, think you don't have the time to serve your patients the way you'd like, are not getting the ratings you believe you deserve, and are not enjoying practicing medicine as you should be and want to be, keep reading. This book is for you.

If you've had a hospital or practice administrator come to you and say, "Your patient satisfaction scores are not high enough, and you need to improve them starting right now," this book is for you.

If you have made the mistake of going online to see what your patients had to say about you on Yelp! or Angie's List, or HealthGrades, or RateMDs and you didn't like what you saw, this book is for you.

If you want to preserve your income, this book is for you.

If there are days you dread going to work, this book is for you.

But most of all, if you are already an excellent practitioner—a doctor, nurse, nurse practitioner, physician's assistant, etc.—with great bedside manner who is always looking for ways to give your patients a better experience and who wants to enjoy practicing more...

This book was written for you.

SECTION I

WHERE WE ARE

CHAPTER 1
THE CHANGING MEDICAL WORLD

SOMETIME AFTER MIDNIGHT ON A frigid winter night near Chicago in the late 1950s, an eight-year-old boy was crying quietly in bed, having been awakened by the pain in his right ear. He knew what it was: yet another ear infection. His mother tried to lower his fever by giving him St. Joseph's Aspirin for Children and sponging his shivering body with diluted rubbing alcohol. She did what she could pending a house call by the family pediatrician, Dr. Elmer Kadison.

Dr. Kadison soon arrived in an overcoat thrown on over his pajamas and bathrobe. The boy's parents later expressed admiration that Dr. Kadison had rushed to their son's bedside without even bothering to get dressed. The doctor seemed not the least put out about coming out in the middle of the night to see yet another sick kid.

He examined the boy carefully and gently, not gagging him with the tongue depressor nor shoving the otoscope too far into his ears, all the while talking to him in a soft voice. From his magical black bag of instruments and cures Dr. Kadison gave the boy a "sucker" to soothe his throat and the parents a bottle of Aureomycin to cure his otitis. The boy felt gratitude and relief and thought, "I want to be like him."

That's why I became a doctor.

Many colleagues have told me similar origin stories of how they were influenced by physicians to become doctors themselves, of how a deep-seated desire to help other people meshed perfectly with a fascination with the biologic sciences or being skilled with their hands or both. How the need to help people, to fix them, to comfort them, drove the proto-physicians to become super-achievers and eventually doctors. And damned good doctors, at that. So why is it that the satisfaction of being a doctor is ebbing? Maybe it's because it seems that everything about medical practice is changing—and not for the better.

The very doctor visit itself has changed. For generations of physicians, while medicine itself evolved constantly, the practice of medicine remained comfortingly steadfast. Aside from the disappearance of the house call, which was once the most common way physicians saw patients ["Jimmy, run get Doc Wilson! Tell him the baby's a-comin'!"], the routine of how patients saw their physicians was unvarying. The patient rode her horse or, for the last century, drove his car to the doctor's office, sat in the waiting room while avoiding eye and germ contact with other ill people, and eventually went into the consultation/ examining room for the face-to-face with the physician. The doctor smiled, chatted a bit, and then asked questions, took inscrutable notes on paper, examined the patient, ruminated, and finally wrote something even less scrutable on a prescription pad. The patient left the doctor, paid the bill with the receptionist, and went off to fill the prescription with the friendly local pharmacist.

Today, everything—except the horse—is the same until you walk into the exam room. Then you are pressed for time. Maybe your employer only allows for a seven-and-a-half-minute office visit. A computer stands interposed between you and the patient. The exam may be more perfunctory. You e-scribe a prescription to the big-box pharmacy-cum-grocery-cum-hardware store that contracts with the patient's insurance plan—if he's lucky enough to have one. The patient leaves a co-pay at the desk or pays in full if he has no insurance plan. And a few weeks later he receives a survey in the mail about his experience with you.

Is that what you thought you were getting into when you became a doctor? Is that how you envisioned your day-to-day life when you dreamed of one day taking care of people?

I think not.

WHAT'S GONE WRONG FOR US

ONCE UPON A TIME, BEING a good physician was enough to virtually guarantee a successful career. In the antediluvian 1980s, when I first went into practice, all one had to do was follow the tenet, often attributed to Sir William Osler, of a new physician's three crucial *A's*: *availability, affability,* and *ability,* in that order. In my new practice, I had plenty of open appointments, lots of time to be nice, and a head full of medical knowledge. My practice grew and thrived. By the time I retired, at age sixty-five, I had long since stopped taking on new patients. There were simply not enough hours in the day nor sufficient ATP in the mitochondria to serve everyone who wanted to see me.*

Today we need to add a fourth *A, adaptability,* because the practice of medicine is undergoing the most radical changes we've seen in our lifetimes:

- Fifteen years ago, 75 percent of American physicians were in private practice and 25 percent were employed by hospitals, health systems like Kaiser Permanente, or the government. Today the percentages are reversed. We've gone from being our own bosses to being cogs in the large, impersonal healthcare machine.
- Electronic health records, supposedly a boon to the practice of medicine, have turned out to be a boon to billers and regulators, but a boondoggle to physicians struggling to record cogent

---

* Osler also said: *My second fixed idea is the uselessness of men above sixty years of age, and the incalculable benefit it would be in commercial, political, and in professional life, if as a matter of course, men stopped work at this age.* I am so done with him.

and succinct histories, physicals, and treatment plans for their patients.

- Patients are rating physicians on the Internet and choosing doctors based on online reviews.
- For more than a century, the model for physician reimbursement was simply fee-for-service: An office visit cost $X. Electrocardiogram, an additional $Y. Lab work, add on $Z. Surgery or procedure, $25X^n$. Within a few years, however, fee-for-service will be gone, to be replaced with I-don't-know-what-and-they-don't-know-what-exactly.

But what *is* known is that what our patients think of us will play a crucial role in whatever the new payment models will be. However our compensation is determined, our patients' satisfaction with their visits with us will be one of the linchpins of our survival. And our survival will depend on our *adaptability*.

WHERE DO WE GO FROM HERE?

FOR MANY DOCTORS, PARTICULARLY THOSE who have been in practice for several years, the future looks discouraging. We face a loss of income, a loss of autonomy, a loss of respect.

For instance, when I joined my practice in 1982, we doctors set the fees we charged. The patients paid at the exit window for the services rendered and received a form to submit to their insurance companies for reimbursement. I once overheard a patient complaining to the senior partner of the practice that insurance would not reimburse the full amount for the visit. I cringed when I heard my partner bluntly reply, "It's your insurance, not mine." But in those days, he was right. With exceptions for people who were financially strapped, our fees were our fees, and that was that.

Now the insurance companies set our fees based on some formula only they know. No discussion, no negotiation. Accept our fees or say goodbye to all your patients that we insure. I realized how bad our insurance reimbursements had become when I discovered that traditionally stingy Medicare had become my highest payer. Since the insurance plans' fees were lower than what we'd previously charged, our incomes dropped.

We physicians have also lost much of our autonomy. In making medical decisions, there was once one principal factor to consider: What was best for the patient. Period. Then, when malpractice suits became increasingly common, we had to start ordering additional tests to protect ourselves from the lawyers and, sadly, from our patients. So we started practicing CYA defensive medicine. And now insurance company functionaries are often the final arbiters of our medical decisions, with ultimate control over what tests we may order and what medications we may prescribe.

Regarding respect, there's an interesting dichotomy between reality and perception. A Harris Poll survey in 2015 found "physician" to be the most respected occupation in the country, with 90 percent of Americans considering doctoring to be a prestigious profession.[1] (This put us ahead of scientists and police officers and way ahead of PR consultants, who placed dead last.) While 90 percent of Americans *would* recommend medicine as a career for their children, 90 percent of physicians *would not*.[2] One of the most common reasons cited by doctors was the feeling that the profession was losing respect.

In a 2011 Consumer Reports study, 70 percent of primary care physicians believed that "since they had started practicing medicine, respect and appreciation from patients had gotten 'a little' or 'much' worse."[3] Doctors regularly complain online about how lack of respect from patients, insurers, and even hospitals makes their jobs harder.[4] One doctor even wrote a powerful memoir about the descent of the profession's image "from knighthood to knavery."[5]

So now what? It's too late to turn back. You're a physician or a surgeon, and short of getting an MBA or going to—heaven forfend!— law school, doctoring is what you are going to do. Until golf sets in.

After all, you've invested nearly half your life becoming a doctor. When you finished your residency or fellowship, you were graduating from between twenty-third and thirtieth grade. Then, and only then, could you start to earn a living while paying off debts. But you knew that you would have a truly fulfilling career and would do a world of good for other people along the way. For many of us, though, it seems as if the personal satisfaction of practicing medicine is slipping away—or, more accurately, being taken from us.

Our profession has become relegated to a position somewhat less than noble. Yes, we are still trusted by the public, ranking third behind only nurses and pharmacists. (And well above lawyers, HMO managers, and members of Congress, I might add.) However, most of us are now employees of hospitals, health systems, HMOs, or Accountable Care Organizations. This renders us interchangeable and, worse, makes us have to answer to people other than our patients. To put it bluntly, we have lost our special place in society's eyes—and in our own eyes.

WE ARE IN THIS TOGETHER

ON THE OLD STONE ENTRANCE to Columbia Presbyterian Medical Center on 168th Street in New York City is carved the biblical inscription *For of the Most High Cometh Healing.* As a medical student at Columbia P&S, seeing those words as I walked to class every day reminded me that I was pursuing not just a job, nor even a career, but a higher calling. The long hours of sometimes tedious study (Do I *really* have to remember the peregrinations of the fifth cranial nerve?) were leading me to fulfill a childhood dream of being a doctor.

For several years that dream was fully realized. I built a thriving private practice with partners I liked and admired. I developed friendships with patients that lasted decades; they called me Dr. Bob. I had families for whom I took care of four generations. I made a good, if not spectacular, living. Then everything started to go downhill.

In the early to mid-1990s my practice, like many of yours, was shaken to the core by "managed care." After the failure of the Bill and Hillary healthcare reform initiative, the insurance companies took over healthcare. Suddenly, some of my long-term patients couldn't see me because their employers had changed insurance plans, and I wasn't on their new panel of "primary care providers." I could not always refer to specialists I knew well and had used for years because they weren't on the same panels as I. And even if they were, I had to get some functionary's permission for a specialist referral. I had been relegated to the role of "gatekeeper." Not what I had dreamed of.

One day I was complaining so much about what was happening in medicine that my fifteen-year-old daughter casually informed me, "Daddy, you have a crappy job." Her precocious perspicacity might explain why today she is a highly-paid business consultant.

Over time, insurance companies became the de facto overlords of medicine. They set fees—my small seven-doctor practice was in no position to bargain with them. The insurance companies required us to get pre-authorizations on routine tests such as CT scans, so we had to add a full-time employee just to get permission to order the tests. The overlords struck deals with pharmaceutical companies to reduce the costs of medications and thus restricted the formularies of medications we could prescribe. We needed to hire another full-time person to work on medication refills and authorizations.

When my prescription maven was unable to get approval for a medication, I had to get on the phone to advocate for my patients and argue with the insurance company representative.

My editor made me remove the several choice epithets I'd written about the people who formulated the policy that led to the following incident:

A young patient of mine, Alex, fresh out of law school, got a new job which provided healthcare insurance (lucky him!) with a different insurance company than he'd had when he was on his parents' plan.

Alex was very bright and personable, but when he was in college he had started having great difficulties with his studies. He underwent neuropsychological testing and was found to have ADHD. The psychologist recommended Vyvanse, which my patient's pediatrician prescribed. Alex's response was excellent. He completed college and law school, passed the bar exam, and joined a prestigious firm in New York City. By then he had outgrown the pediatrician and had been my patient for a year.

However, when Alex went to his pharmacy to pick up a refill of his Vyvanse, he was told that the medication was not covered by his new insurance company. The pharmacist told him that he had to try other medications first.

I put Marie, my prescription maven, on the case, and she promptly hit a brick wall. The insurance company representative told her that Alex would have to *try and fail on* three other medications before they would approve the Vyvanse. I got on the phone and got no further with the representative than Marie had.

So I asked for the supervisor and got no further with her. Finally, after days of phone calls, I reached the company's medical director. Initially he reiterated the policy to me. I said, "If you make this man try three other medications, suppose they don't work? By your rules, he's going to have to try one after the other until *maybe* he finds one that helps his condition. But while the medications are failing, his career could fall apart." Fortunately, the medical director saw the merit in this argument and approved the Vyvanse—for a year.

And with another patient, this conversation really happened. Really.

Me: Hello, this is Dr. Baker. Who is this, please?
Jones: This is Mr. Jones from the formulary department. How can I help you?
Me: Thank you, Mr. Jones, for taking the call. I'm calling about my patient Mrs. Jean Connolly...
Jones: Cannoli?

Me: No, Mrs. Connolly. I recently started her on 100 mg of a new diabetes medication, but it wasn't controlling her sugar well enough, so I raised the dose to two 100 mg tablets a day, but her plan wouldn't cover that.
Jones: That's right. We cover one 100 mg tablet.
Me: But she needs 200 mg.
Jones: We don't cover two 100 mg tablets a day.
Me: But in my medical judgment that's what she needs. [That should do it, right?]
Jones: There is a 300 mg tablet. We do cover that.
Me: I understand, but I'm concerned that 300 mg might make her hypoglycemic.
Jones: Then prescribe the 100 mg.
Me: I did that, but it wasn't enough. I want her to try 200 mg.
Jones: We don't cover that.
Me: I know you don't cover that, but that's what the patient needs.
Jones: 100 mg or 300 mg, doctor, that's what we cover.
Me: I understand that, but I've known her for fifteen years, and I think…
Jones: Is there anything else I can help you with today, doctor?
Me: [unprintable]

Yeah, that's why I went to school for all those years and missed all the fun my friends were having. So I could do *that*.

As the pressures on our practice grew, we decided to merge with the local hospital, which has since grown into a major health system. When I retired, I had gone from being one of seven internists in an intimate practice to one of two thousand physician employees. After I left, a new doctor was brought into the practice to take my place.

REVIEWS? WE DON'T NEED NO STINKIN' REVIEWS!

Word-of-mouth built my practice. But now we're all subject to word-of-net. A study published in *Medical Economics*[6] showed that 77 percent of patients will look at online reviews when selecting a new physician. If you've never looked yourself up on the Internet (in which case you're smarter than I), go check your ratings on HealthGrades.com, or Yelp!, Angie's List, RateMDs.com, vitals.com, or CareDash.com, to name a few. You may be pleasantly—or unpleasantly—surprised. Probably some of both. Go ahead and look. I'll wait right here for you.

Recovered? Try a few deep breaths. It can help.

Most patient online reviews around the country are positive. In 2013, Vanguard Communications studied ratings of over forty-three thousand providers in the one hundred largest US cities. About 57 percent of the doctors received four stars or better.[7]

Nevertheless, the problems with online review sites are legion.[8] The greatest is that reviews are statistically insignificant—wildly so. The second biggest problem is that potential patients don't know that and believe that such reviews accurately reflect reality. Look, if two of three people who've posted reviews give you five out of five stars and one angry person gives you one star, you average out to three and two-thirds stars. So anyone online scanning a list of doctors in their area is going to find you way down below all the four- and five-star doctors—if they even bother to plunge that far into the depths of the list.

This exact scenario happened to me. On one site, I had two lovely reviews and one from a patient who wrote three paragraphs hating on my office. She had waited a long time for an appointment for a shingles shot only to find out on her arrival at the office that we had run out of vaccine. Unfortunately, no one had called her to reschedule her appointment, and she was angry, which I completely understand. But the one-star rating she gave me dragged me down near the bottom of the list of doctors in my area.

One infrequently cited problem with online reviews is that they can undermine current patients' confidence in us. Don't we sometimes look up restaurants we frequent or cars we drive to see the reviews? What do our patients think if they see we have less than stellar ratings? Maybe a low score eats into their confidence in us. It can even chip away at our confidence in our colleagues.

I once had a patient complain to me that he had looked up a neurologist I had referred him to before making an appointment with the doctor. "How could you send me to that guy?" he asked. "Have you seen his reviews?" I hadn't. Why would I look up the reviews of someone I knew to be an excellent practitioner?

I wanted to say, "Whom are you going to believe, me—your doctor—or your lying eyes?" Instead, I explained that I had been sending patients to the neurologist for twenty years and had never had a complaint from a patient. The denouement? My patient did not see that neurologist. Nor did he see me ever again.

There's plenty of advice available about how to deal with negative online reviews.* For instance, the health system I worked for gave doctors a chance to challenge critical patient comments before posting them on our profiles on the system's website. There are businesses that help doctors manage their online reputations.[9] What concerns me more, however, is how to prevent bad reviews in the first place, how to deliver such an excellent patient experience that no one would think of giving you a less than five-star review. That's what this book is about.

As if online reviews from patients weren't enough to worry about, consider this: It's not just the patients who are looking at our reviews. The payers are, too. The Centers for Medicare and Medicaid Services (CMS), Kaiser, the Blues, and United Health Care all have pilot programs examining using patient satisfaction scores to help determine physician compensation.

As I mentioned before, fee-for-service is going away. Someone realized that if you reward practitioners for doing more, they'll do more—not necessarily more than is needed, but certainly more. Now those same someones have decided that this current mode of physician reimbursement is unsustainable. In casting about for other payment models, they've decided that it's better to reward quality than quantity. So they've come up with "quality measures," which CMS defines as

---
* I especially like *Hug Your Haters* by Jay Baer. New York: Portfolio/Penguin, 2016.

"tools that help us measure or quantify healthcare processes, outcomes, *patient perceptions* [emphasis added], and organizational structure and/or systems that are associated with the ability to provide high-quality health care…"

We are being bombarded by a torrent of acronyms—MACRA, MDP, EMA, QCDR, MIPS, APMs, ACOs, PFPMs—which may or may not be in place a few years from now. And those are just from CMS. Who knows what future pleasures the insurance companies have planned for us?

Therefore, I'm going to ignore all that *chazerai*. For our purposes, I'm going to assume, as I noted earlier, that you are an excellent clinician, and that your "healthcare processes and outcomes" are already excellent. In fact, you probably assume that, too, since studies show that two-thirds of us physicians consider ourselves to be better than average doctors.

Instead, let's concentrate on the "patient perception" piece. Now it's uncertain how much of our reimbursement will eventually be based on patient satisfaction scores, but according to Francois de Brantes, executive director of the Health Care Incentives Improvement Institute, it should be as much as "a solid third."[10] And that approximately 30 percent does not exist in isolation, since studies show that improved patient satisfaction leads to improved patient compliance,[11] which, of course, affects that other 70 percent—the quality measures.

As we'd expect, physicians are not happy with the prospect of patient surveys affecting their salaries.[12] Why would we want to change a system that has rewarded us well for decades? Moreover, surveys could be subject to bias, manipulation, and averaging,* to say nothing of patient spite.

---

* For instance, when I looked myself up on Medicare's "Physician Compare" website, I was stunned by my poor performance scores. One example: I'm an internist/gastroenterologist, and my colorectal screening score was reported at an abysmal 67 percent. Then I saw that Medicare was actually reporting the results of the two thousand physicians in multiple specialties (including psychiatrists and orthopedists) who work for my employer. I was lumped in with everybody, so I'm guessing those orthopedists pulled my colon-cancer-screening score down.

Yeah, well, too bad, doctors. The new reimbursement model is happening,[13] so we need to figure out what we can do to improve our personal patient satisfaction scores. The good news is, it's easy to do consistently and ethically. And, as you'll see, with greater *physician* satisfaction scores.

What we need is a path back to those emotions that made us want to become doctors in the first place, a way to experience them every day at work, no matter how stressful our day or what outside forces conspire to make us unhappy. We need to rekindle our love of our profession, to reignite the passion that made us devote half our lives to becoming physicians.

Think of your own origin story; I'm sure you have one. Somewhere inside the tired, beleaguered, discouraged, current-day you is the young woman or man who dreamed of being a doctor, who sacrificed seemingly endlessly to become one of the select group of people who are privileged to take care of other people, to join the ranks of those from whom "cometh healing."

Despite all the pressures we face, there is a way to enjoy practicing medicine every day, and to have the personal satisfaction that being a doctor should bring. There is. That is to focus on the only aspect of patient experience that we can control—our direct face-to-face encounters with our patients. We do that by performing our best when we see patients.

TAKEAWAYS

- The practice of medicine is undergoing the most radical changes of our lifetimes.
- Doctors face a loss of income, autonomy, and respect.
- Many physicians are unhappy with their choice of profession.
- As fee-for-service vanishes, quality and patient experience will come to the fore.
- The only thing we can directly control is the patient encounter.

CHAPTER 2
THE PATIENT VISIT IS A PERFORMANCE

LISSENCEPHALY. DO YOU REMEMBER WHAT it is? I didn't. I was far enough removed from medical school lectures on disorders of fetal neuronal migration that, when my new patient, Mrs. Enescu,* told me that her three-year-old daughter had it, I had to nod sagely and then dash to my office and look it up while Mrs. E. was changing into a gown for her exam.

The word lissencephaly comes from the Greek for "smooth brain" because the cerebral cortex develops in utero with either small (pachygyria) or no (agyria) gyri, the brain surface's folds and convolutions. Children with this condition have a variety of disorders of variable severity, including psychomotor delay, seizures, feeding and swallowing difficulties, and respiratory abnormalities from frequent aspiration.

Mrs. Enescu's daughter, Sarah, has agyria and lives at home on a respirator with twenty-four-hour nursing care provided by her mother because insurance won't cover... well, that's another issue. Mrs. Enescu gave up a high-powered corporate job in New York City to tend to her daughter. Mr. Enescu is a scientist at a physics laboratory which is generous in the time it allows him to work from home to relieve his wife.

---

*Not her real name, of course.

Sarah herself has a small head with lots of curly hair, sparkling eyes, and a sweet, sweet smile. She sits propped up in her hospital bed with a favorite stuffed mouse as her constant companion. I know because her mom always brings pictures to show me. In the photos, Mrs. E. had arranged Sarah's clothes to hide her tracheostomy and jejunostomy tubes. The photos don't show that now five-year-old Sarah functions at the level of an infant.

Mrs. Enescu is unremittingly positive and upbeat about Sarah. I understand this, as I am the father of two children on the autism spectrum. Positivity and hope for our children is what gets us through each day. However, my children have a normal life expectancy. Sarah's does not extend much beyond ten years.

One day, after she'd been my patient for a few years, Mrs. Enescu came in for a routine blood pressure check. As I always did, I started our visit asking about Sarah, and her face fell.

"Oh, Dr. Baker, it's terrible," she said. "Sarah just spent three weeks in the pediatric ICU with uncontrollable seizures. The doctors tried all sorts of different medications, but before they found the right combination, her feeding tube fell out, and she developed pneumonia. She almost died, but finally they let us bring her home.

"We know it is for the last time."

Suddenly, Mrs. Enescu's blood pressure was not the main focus of her visit. I felt a flood of sadness and loss fill me to my brimming eyes. We hugged. We cried. We looked at pictures. I supported her as best I could.

And eventually I checked her blood pressure.

But then I was twenty-five minutes late for my next patient, who was a nice, middle-aged lady coming in for a routine physical. I didn't know how I was going to get through it. I felt emotionally, even physically, drained.

So I gathered myself, stood outside the exam room door, put my hand on the knob, and heard myself say under my breath, "Robert, it's showtime." I stood up straight so I'd have energy, put on my warmest, friendliest smile so I'd feel good, opened that door, and performed a really good, empathic history and physical. And for the rest of the day, I felt much better. I had performed well for my patient.

PERFORM THE RITUAL

THAT EPISODE COALESCED, FOR ME, an idea I'd had for a long time: that when a doctor sees a patient at the bedside, or in a consulting office, or in an exam room, it's a performance. That's right, a performance.

When I've propounded this idea to doctors, some nod in agreement, but many seem scandalized, or at least annoyed at my effrontery. After all, isn't a doctor the *opposite* of a performer? A doctor is a clinician, a scientist. A doctor is genuine, caring, and empathic—certainly not a performer, certainly not a *fake*!

However, my contention that the doctor visit is a performance makes a lot of sense with a definition of *performance* that takes it out of the show business context. According to Erving Goffman, considered by many to be the most influential American sociologist of the twentieth century, a *"performance" may be defined as all the activity of a given participant on a given occasion which serves to influence in some way any of the other participants.*[1] And then there's what Shakespeare said about the world being a stage.

I started to formulate this idea of the patient encounter being a performance very early in my practice thanks to one of my senior partners, Dr. Michael Cohen, an eminent and immensely popular physician in our community. You see, when I first went into practice, I had no idea what to expect. I had trained in the academic centers of Columbia, Cornell, and Harvard and so had a very skewed idea of the spectrum of human illness.

For instance, from my GI fellowship at Beth Israel Medical Center in Boston, I had concluded that the most common gastrointestinal ailments in the population were inflammatory bowel disease, primary biliary cholangitis, Laennec's cirrhosis, and major gastrointestinal bleeding of various etiologies. Oh, and the occasional infectious diarrhea.

So imagine my surprise when I ended up in private practice in the Long Island suburbs of New York City and saw only inflammatory bowel disease from the above list. I did see lots of gastroesophageal reflux, dyspepsia, and irritable bowel syndrome. Where the hell did they come from?

I was so distressed that after a month I called my mentor at Beth Israel, Dr. Mark Peppercorn, to complain about the narrow spectrum of diseases I was seeing. He laughed and said, "That's what outpatient GI is!" Oh.

To add to the July of my discontent, I was also doing general internal medicine, something no self-respecting, academically trained, third-year GI fellow would be caught dead doing today. So besides the folks with belching, heartburn, and constipation, I was also seeing kvetchy people with upper respiratory infections and raging fevers of 99.3 ("I usually run below normal."). My patients were quick to educate me that this medical situation required a Z-Pak. Phoned in now!

After I'd been in my new practice for a few months, my partner Michael came into my consulting office to tell me that he was receiving complaints about me from his patients who had been stuck seeing me when he was already booked. They were telling him that I wasn't taking their complaints seriously enough.

He suggested that I take a more thorough history and perform a more detailed physical examination. He showed me how to use a special light we had for transilluminating sinuses to look for opacification in patients with URI symptoms. Dr. Cohen also suggested I show the patients some *rachmones*, Yiddish for compassion.

At first, this really annoyed me. I said, "Are you kidding me? You want me to treat a head cold like a serious medical problem?"

He gently responded, "If they're taking time out of their days to see you, for them it *is* serious." Michael reminded me that the patients might be concerned that their symptoms represented something more threatening than just a cold, or that they might just have wanted my assistance to feel better and return to their normal lives. Okay, I got that.

But then he said something that initiated the change in how I thought about the patient encounter. He pointed out that the doctor visit is a kind of ritual involving an authority figure wearing a costume (white coat), the telling of a story, and the laying on of hands. Supplicants even receive an amulet in the form of a prescription. He added, "Patients expect that we will perform the ritual in its entirety and seriously and they won't be satisfied if we don't."

"Perform the ritual." The words resonated with me. "Perform the ritual." Then I had a junior-associate flash of intuition. The ritual is a vital part of the healing process. How else to explain what I bet you've heard many times from patients departing from a visit: "You know, doc, I feel better already!"

It's wonderful, right? Because we haven't done anything, except *perform the ritual*. And patients expect that we will perform it. It was then that I realized that, when a doctor sees a patient in the exam room, or at the bedside, or in the consulting office, it is a *performance*. And, as we'll see, a good performance produces a better result for both doctor and patient.

But first, we'd better address the issue of performances being somehow fake or inauthentic. Such an assumption presumes that the performance is superimposed on, and not part of, the performer's genuine thoughts or feelings.

Michael Port, the author of the seminal *Steal the Show*,[2] succinctly addresses this notion in a single sentence:

> *Good performance is authentic behavior*
> *in a manufactured environment.*

Please read that again, and we'll break it down.

By "manufactured environment," Port means a situation which is created for a specific purpose. He's a trained actor, so for him a manufactured environment might be a stage or a movie set. When we see two characters in a movie talking in their home's living room, that living room is merely a set designed to simulate a living room—a manufactured environment. But a lawyer speaking in a courtroom is also in a manufactured environment. It's real life, but the setup is created as a place for the law to come to life.

For us, calling a doctor's visit a manufactured environment might seem a stretch. After all, it's what we do every day, so nothing seems "manufactured." But for the patient, everything is. First, they have to drive to a place created for the purpose of doctoring. Then they have to answer questions about very personal things. Finally, they must undress to have their bodies poked and prodded by a near-stranger. It's totally outside their everyday experience.

And then, Michael Port says that in good performance behavior is authentic. How do actors make a performance authentic? They do it by committing to the characters they are playing and to the reality of the situations the characters find themselves in. They also do it by showing themselves to be human and vulnerable.[3]

This is exactly what we need to do as physicians to establish rapport with our patients and to get maximum therapeutic benefit from the visit. We need to act authentically and be fully committed to the situation. We also need to let our humanity and vulnerability show.

Now, you might be thinking, "I'm not an actor." Well, neither am I. But I know you have performing experience. Perhaps you appeared in your fifth-grade elementary school play. You may or may not have been stellar, but it was a performance. Maybe you've offered a toast at a wedding. You had to get up in front of a group of people, many of them strangers, and give a speech that was humorous and meaningful to the bride and groom. Perhaps you've given a speech honoring a retiring colleague. Both were performances.

When you interviewed for college or medical school or even your current job, you had to present the best version of yourself to the interviewer. You had to be your best you. In those interviews, your behavior was authentically you; but still, those were performances.

Or how about the time one of your kids used that perfectly placed curse word? It was hilarious, right? But you couldn't laugh (unless you're a lousy parent like me). You had to play the role of stern and disapproving parent. You put on a performance.

If you stop and think about it, life is full of authentic performances. When a lawyer summarizes a case before a jury, that's a performance.* When an airline pilot comes on the intercom to give a reassuring preflight announcement, she is playing the role of her best pilot self. It's authentic, but it's a performance. When an expert waiter gives excellent service at a restaurant, he's bringing his skills and knowledge to provide a wonderful dining experience. That's a performance.

Great performances involve the audience and produce genuine emotions in them. And we want to produce emotions in our patients because, to paraphrase a quotation attributed to Maya Angelou, our patients will forget what we said, and they'll forget what we did, but they'll never forget how we made them feel.†

Now, what about every time you see a patient at the bedside or in an exam room or in your consulting office? If you look carefully at yourself in those situations, I'm guessing that you can see elements of your behavior, language, personality, mannerisms, and even physicality that aren't a part of your life anywhere else. I submit that what you are doing there *is* a performance. You've been doing it for years, but probably not consciously. This book aims to raise your performance from unconscious to purposeful to five-star patient experience.

And there's no fakery involved, because the part you are playing is yourself. Not your hassled, worried-about-the-mortgage,

---

* Okay, maybe I shouldn't use that as an appealing example for doctors.
† She was herself paraphrasing an earlier quotation from Carl Buehner: "They may forget what you said — but they will never forget how you made them feel."

running-behind-schedule self. Rather, you are playing your physician self. This is different from your parent self, or your soccer coach self, or your going-out-to-eat-with-friends self. Each of these, including your doctor self, is an integral part of you.

To repeat the wisdom of Shakespeare in *As You Like It*, "All the world's a stage, And all the men and women merely players... And one man in his time plays many parts."[4]

Sixty years ago, Erving Goffman analyzed this idea further in his seminal work *The Presentation of Self in Everyday Life*, in which he demonstrated how we show the world different aspects of ourselves depending on the circumstances we are in.[5] In addition, he showed that our performances are an expression of our own identities.

We'll learn more from Goffman later, but what I'm asking you to do in this book is to consider every patient encounter to be a performance, one that is an authentic expression of your true self. I'll show you the skills, techniques, and strategies that will enable you to make every patient interaction a stellar performance.

WHY SHOULD I BOTHER?

You probably pride yourself on your bedside manner. Especially if you've been doctoring for a number of years and have a successful practice, you're confident you have that part nailed down. And you may feel that you don't need some gastroenterologist/ventriloquist telling you how to behave with your patients. Well, as Dr. James Merlino, formerly the chief experience officer of the Cleveland Clinic, puts it, "There's an important, significant disconnect between how we as providers think we communicate with patients and how patients rate our ability to communicate... If you ask physicians to rate themselves on patient communication, they'll say they are excellent and that they have excellent patient relationships."[6]

I'd add that even the greatest tennis player of all time, Roger Federer, has a coach. Mariano Rivera, the greatest relief pitcher of all time, worked every day with a pitching coach. Every little bit that they upped their games helped their performances. Furthermore, treating every patient encounter as a performance has benefits for both you and your patients.

IT STARTS THE PROCESS OF HEALING.

I believe in my heart that the magic of healing begins when a doctor and patient sit down together and start to talk. Everything else we bring to the encounter—our technical prowess, our smarts, our fund of knowledge—is of little use if we don't understand the patient's medical issues and concerns and if we don't communicate that understanding to him or her.

As I said in the Introduction, the goal of any performance is to *connect with* and *communicate with* an audience, in this case your patient. By employing the skills and techniques that great performers use, we can greatly enhance that communication, make that connection, win the patient's trust, and give him faith in our competence and dedication to his care.

IT HELPS YOU TO FOCUS ON THE PATIENT.

The distractions of daily medical practice are many: the seemingly unending stream of telephone calls from patients, requests for refills, drug company reps who want to bribe you with lunch, interruptions by staff, forms waiting to be filled out, knowledge that the next patient is waiting, perhaps for too long, and on and on.

Now, some people believe that they can multitask. Research indicates, however, that our perceptions of our ability to do several things or think and deal with several problems simultaneously are "badly inflated" with "little grounding in reality."[7] For instance, we may think that we can drive and talk on the phone simultaneously, but research shows that doing so impairs our driving to the same degree as ethanol intoxication.[8]

Dr. Theo Tsaousides, the author of *Brain Blocks*, puts it this way: "While your brain can handle multiple things at once in the background [controlling breathing, regulating body temperature], it can handle only one thing at a time in the foreground. You can be doing several things at once, but you can pay attention to only one of them."[9]

Finally, we'll discuss in Chapter 7 how being in performance mode allows—no, demands—that you are fully present with the patient, paying attention only to the person in the room with you. This enables to you perform at your peak as a physician.

A GOOD PERFORMANCE ENHANCES EMPATHY.

Being fully present requires that we listen and observe, and these actions are essential to a good performance. They activate the mirror neurons in the premotor cortex and inferior parietal cortex. One theory is that this mirroring is the physiologic basis for empathy,[10] so crucial to being a great physician and connecting with patients. The greater the empathy we have for our patients, the better their experiences with us will be. We'll see specific examples of how performance creates empathy later.

THE WORKDAY GOES BY FASTER.

Most performers experience a time warp onstage. I know I do. When I am speaking to doctors and am in the "full flow" of giving my talk, I completely lose track of time, at least consciously. I somehow always know when my speaking time is up, but while I'm onstage, there is no time, and I'm amazed afterward how short the performance seems in retrospect. I found the same thing seeing patients in the office. Being in performance mode can make what promised to be a long, stressful day feel afterward as if it had flown by in a flash. The feeling was almost exhilarating.

PERFORMING IS FUN.

If you're a musician, dancer, actor, or stand-up comic (yes, there are some docs who do that), you already know that performing is fun. If you've ever been in a school play, sung in a church choir, played in a rock band, or told jokes to friends, you already know that performing is fun. Performing music—not merely listening to it—releases endorphins.[11] I'm sure that's true of performing comedy or public speaking as well. Invariably, the first thought that goes through my mind after a successful speech is, "Where can I get more of *that*?" And after a good day of medical performance, I'm eager to come back to work the next day. How often do you feel that?

MAKING YOUR VISIT A PERFORMANCE SATISFIES PATIENTS.
Surveys show that there are just a few things that patients want from their doctor visits. To understand how a good performance satisfies those desires, we'll turn to them shortly.

TAKEAWAYS

- In our lives, we have many selves and perform many roles.
- When we see patients, we are being the biggest, best version of our physician selves.
- Good performance is authentic behavior in a manufactured environment.
- A good performance enhances empathy.
- A performance is enjoyable.
- Making your visit a performance satisfies patients.

CHAPTER 3
I'M NOT A PERFORMER AND DON'T WANT TO BE

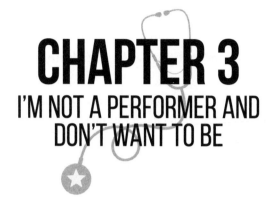

I GET IT. YOU'RE SKEPTICAL. Besides, you're not interested in becoming a performer, and I understand how you might feel that way. Here are other concerns you might raise to me:

- *Medicine is a serious life and death business, and you're trivializing it.*
- *I have enough to think about when I'm with a patient. Now you want me to perform?*
- *I'm shy or an introvert. Dealing with people saps my energy as it is.*
- *I see thirty patients a day. I don't have time for this.*
- *Other businesses don't use performance techniques.*
- *How do you know your approach works?*
- *You're a ventriloquist.*

All fair objections.

I am not in the least bit interested in turning you into a performer. Nor do I believe that you need to become one to improve the patient experience. However, I maintain that lessons I've learned from the stage do transmogrify into techniques and strategies that can be used with patients. No matter what your personal style and proclivities, you can apply what's in this book to your daily interactions with patients.

Transferability of skills is common. You may not be a C-suite executive, but that doesn't mean that you can't apply some of Steven Covey's 7 *Habits of Highly Effective People* to both your work life and your personal life.

You may have had a "liberal arts" college education, very little of which you directly use in your daily medical practice. However, there is consensus that a solid grounding in the liberal arts makes for a better physician. For instance, Missouri State University says on its website that, for premedical students, "The aim of a liberal arts education is insight, understanding, imagination, and discovery; defining one's unique self, one's values, and one's place in the world."[1]

Further, Wellesley College says, in its Mission and Values statement, "Mastery of a broad range of intellectual and cultural content lends crucial perspective to any decision-making. Wellesley cultivates an avid curiosity and the willingness to interrogate closely, argue cogently, and judge fairly; as well as an awareness that allows the drawing of ethical lines clearly, cleanly, and publicly."[2] Surely these are skills that would stand a physician in good stead.

One of the most prestigious medical schools in the country, The Ichan School of Medicine at Mount Sinai Hospital in New York City, actually has a program to recruit humanities majors to become medical students there.

My point is that, just because a skill set or knowledge base is not *directly* applicable to patient interactions, that does not mean those skills cannot be applied to the medical setting.

★   ★   ★

YOU ARE TRIVIALIZING MEDICINE.

I contend that treating the patient visit as a performance does not trivialize it, but rather elevates it. To perform effectively on stage, the performer has to be fully dedicated to the performance, to be "all in." In recent years, the magician David Copperfield has been criticized in the magic literature (yes, we do have a literature!) for "phoning in" his performances, meaning that he seemed to be disinterested in his shows and was just going through the motions without relating to his audiences. Recently, however, he revamped his show, adding new illusions and bringing a renewed enthusiasm to his performances. Audiences and magician critics have noticed, as did I when I saw him recently in Las Vegas.

A performer must be at his best for every performance because every audience is new. For us, every next patient is a new audience for whom we must perform at our best.

★   ★   ★

I HAVE ENOUGH TO THINK ABOUT AS IT IS.

Yes, there is plenty to keep in mind when seeing a patient: everything we know about the patient's past medical history and current problems. What tests have been done and which need to be performed.* What's my diagnostic and therapeutic plan? What do I need to discuss with the family? How's the office running today? Did lunch come yet?

So it may seem that thinking about performance techniques would be an additional burden on the busy physician's brain. It's true that adding new techniques to your repertoire may at first feel a little forced or unnatural. I liken the feeling to that a baseball player might have making a coach's suggested adjustments to his batting swing. Initially, the new swing feels uncomfortable, even wrong, compared to what the player has been doing for years. But very soon the new swing becomes second nature, and the player's hitting improves.

It's the same with the strategies and techniques we'll be discussing. They may at first require some conscious thought and conscious, though minimal, effort to put them to use. However, they will soon

---

* There's that word again!

become your usual practices, and you'll employ them without even thinking about them.

★   ★   ★

I'M SHY OR INTROVERTED.

Nothing wrong with that. I am, too. Take me to a party where I don't know anyone, and you'll soon find me off to the side of the room nursing a club soda with lime. It's very difficult for me to walk up to a stranger and start talking to him. What am I supposed to say? When I go to medical conferences, I have to really force myself to strike up conversations with people, even when it is greatly to my advantage to do so.

Yet, strange as it may seem, that natural reticence does not affect my ability to perform onstage. I'm completely comfortable speaking to or performing for hundreds or even thousands of people. I know how to engage the whole audience; it's the one-on-one that I find challenging. In the office, though, I have no difficulty because even if I've never met the patient before, we both know what our roles are before I walk in the door. They are expecting to meet Dr. Baker, so I can become my doctor self and perform that role comfortably and well.

Not being able to do that can affect how patients react to you. A friend of mine is a superb dermatologist, but some patients I've referred to him have refused to go back, saying that he barely speaks to them or that he's unfriendly.

He's not unfriendly, but, as he's told me, he would rather have been a researcher and an academic dermatologist. He went into practice, I suspect, for financial reasons. If he were to adopt just two of the skills we'll discuss—smiling and making eye contact—I'm certain that the people who see him would have a different reaction.

The same could apply to you. The performance techniques we'll discuss are easy to implement and require no extra time on your part.

You don't even have to try all of them. Still, they could easily become part of your "natural swing."

★ ★ ★

I DON'T HAVE TIME IN MY BUSY DAY TO DO THIS.
The vast majority of the techniques and strategies we'll discuss will not add a minute more to your already hectic day. That's a promise.

★ ★ ★

OTHER BUSINESSES DON'T USE PERFORMANCE TECHNIQUES.
Actually, they do. Consider the company with the best customer service in the world: The Walt Disney Company. At their theme parks, all employees, not just the entertainers, are called "cast members."

When a "cast member" is about to enter the active area of a park from "backstage," at the door is a mirror with a reminder to smile and look good because he or she is about to go "on." The employee guideline booklet, *The Disney Look*, for Walt Disney World in Florida reads, "No matter where you work or what your role is, anytime you are in a public area, you are 'on stage.' Your attitude and performance are direct reflections on the quality of our Disney show. Often it is the seemingly little things that detract from our guests' enjoyment—chewing gum, having poor posture, using a cellular phone or frowning... All of this adds up to one of the most important aspects of your role in our show: good stage presence."[3]

In a different realm, consider the business of teaching. Think back on some of very best teachers you had in your academic career, the ones who inspired you, who made seemingly boring subjects interesting, who did more than just present the material, whose classes seemed to fly by, whom you knew cared about every student in their classes.

I think you'd agree that when they were in front of the class, they were performing, using every technique they knew to engage you. They could "read" the classroom, know who was understanding the lesson and who wasn't, and adjust their performances accordingly. The best teachers have always been great performers.

I remember my developmental psychology class in college. Back then I wanted to be a pediatrician, so the class was potentially very important and interesting to me. The professor, who shall remain nameless, would walk to the front of the lecture room, read a lecture word-for-word from his notes, and walk out. Excruciating. Interest-crushing.

But then there were my chemistry and physics professors, Drs. Hubert Alyea and Eric Rogers. They knew that most of the students in their freshman classes were there because they had to be in order to fulfill requirements. So the professors worked overtime to make their subjects come alive, even to entertain the frosh, and they were consistently among the most popular professors at Princeton.

To return to the world of business, here is an example of a business owner applying lessons he learned from show business to create a multimillion-dollar company. My friend Ken Weber has for the last thirty years been the president of Weber Asset Management, a registered-investment-advisor firm. Ken started his business with zero clients and now manages over three hundred million dollars of other people's money. For seventeen years before he started his investment business, he was a full-time mentalist (magician who performs mind-reading) and stage hypnotist successfully working the college circuit and corporate events.

In discussing how he applies performance techniques to his investment business, Ken told me, "In show business you are successful only if you focus on the end user—your audience—and it's the same thing in my financial business.

"There are a lot of people who are smarter than me, who have greater academic financial backgrounds than I do, but they don't know how to focus on the needs of the client. They will tell the client what the stock market is doing in a very detailed way, all the time missing what the needs of the client are. In show business, I had to learn to watch and listen to the audience. If I didn't meet their needs for the forty-five minutes to hour-and-a-half that I'm onstage, I didn't have a career."

(Ken had to engage his audience for forty-five to ninety minutes. We have to do it for only fifteen to thirty minutes. We can do that!)

Ken continued: "The end user is the same whether I'm onstage talking to a thousand college kids or I'm talking to my client in a conference room. I have to pay attention to what's happening in front of me. If I focus inwardly because I have a wonderful product or service to sell them, I'm going to lose them. I have to focus outwardly. I have to focus on what I see and hear in front of me."

In the doctoring business we need to do this, too. We all know physicians who have superlative credentials and training, but whose bedside manner turns patients off. And in training I can remember doctors on the staff of my hospital who were not academic stars, but good, solid physicians with great "bedside manner," whom anyone would want as a personal doctor.

Techniques performers use to focus on their audience can work for us too. In Chapter 7 we'll examine specific, easily implemented procedures to let our end users—our patients—know we are focused on them.

★   ★   ★

HOW DO YOU KNOW THIS APPROACH WILL WORK FOR ME?

I don't. I'm confident it will, but I can't offer you studies, except one with an N-of-1. Before I started actively applying the techniques I'm writing about, my Press Ganey scores were very respectable. I was in the low- or mid-ninetieth percentiles in every category. In the year that I began practicing what I preach, I climbed to the ninety-ninth percentile in every category,* except that I needed to a little better at talking about meds with patients.

CARE PROVIDER	PERCENTILE
Friendliness/courtesy of CP	99
CP explanations of prob/condition	99
CP concern for questions/worries	99
CP efforts to include in decisions	99
CP information about medications	96
CP instructions for follow-up care	99
CP spoke using clear language	99
Time CP spent with patient	99
Patients' confidence in CP	99
Likelihood of recommending CP	99

Your results may vary, but if you conscientiously work at improving the performance aspects of your patient encounters, I bet they'll start to feel different to you. I believe the "vibe" you get from patients will be better, and their compliance with your recommendations will improve. I even bet that your patient satisfaction scores will rise, and that you'll enjoy seeing patients more. Let me know.

★   ★   ★

---

* However, after I announced my retirement, my "Likelihood to Recommend" numbers dropped. After all, who's going to recommend a doctor who soon won't be there?

YOU'RE A VENTRILOQUIST!

Guilty as charged. But that doesn't make me strange. When I perform "vent," as we call it, I'm an actor playing two parts simultaneously with the pure and simple goal of making people laugh, have a good time, and forget about their problems for a while. I want them to walk out of my show feeling good.

And out of my office, too.

So, I ask that you put aside your skepticism and objections and try the things I'm going to suggest. I think you'll be pleasantly surprised. If you have any other reservations or concerns, please email me at Bob@ThePerformanceOfMedicine.com.

TAKEAWAYS

- You don't have to be a performer to give a good performance.
- You can try the techniques in this book without consciously thinking you're performing.
- Successful businesses use the "performance" model to give great customer service.
- Ventriloquists are cool.

CHAPTER 4
WHAT PATIENTS WANT

AFTER LISTENING TO THIRTY-FIVE YEARS of patient complaints about my own office, I've been able to figure out exactly what patients want to experience when they go to see a doctor...

A cheerful, calm secretary picks up the phone on the second, or at worst third, ring. The office telephone system does not have a HOLD button. The patient asks for an appointment to see his particular physician and, as usual, she has an appointment available for the exact date and time the patient wants to be seen. No negotiation is necessary, and there's no need to see one of the other doctors, or, heaven forfend, the NP in the office.

The patient arrives at the practice's clean, modern office building where there is a convenient parking spot steps away from the entrance. When he enters the soothingly decorated office, the patient is greeted by a bright, cheerful secretary who knows him, has apparently been eagerly awaiting his arrival, and checks him in immediately. There are no superfluous, repetitive forms to fill out because the receptionist has intuited that none of his information has changed.

The patient sits in the nearly empty waiting room and, before he can grab a crisp, current magazine, a cheerful, untroubled medical assistant calls his name to come in. She, too, seems delighted to see him.

The assistant escorts the patient to a spotless examination room and asks him to take off his shirt and slip on a luxurious cloth gown; she steps outside the room while he changes. The assistant lingers outside the door of the room, awaiting his signal to reenter.

The medical assistant expertly takes the patient's vital signs, pumping the BP cuff to just the right level—not too tight. She taps these into the EHR system and informs the patient that the doctor will be right in. She has hardly left when the doctor knocks and enters the room, clearly overjoyed to see him. "I must be one of her favorite patients," he congratulates himself.

The unhurried doctor apparently has no other patients to see that day, or at least none as important as he. She inquires about his family, shares a humorous anecdote about her own, and then takes a brief, but thorough, history regarding the reason for his visit. She performs an expert examination made comfortable by the warm stethoscope she applies to his skin. Nothing hurts when she palpates.

The doctor asks the patient to get dressed and steps out. She, too, lingers outside the exam room door, waiting for him to change.

Reentering the room, the doctor explains thoroughly, yet succinctly, exactly what the medical problem is. She expresses none of the "it could be this or it could be that" uncertainty he has experienced with other physicians. No further testing is necessary, since she knows exactly what is going on. She tells him she will transmit a prescription to his pharmacy immediately; it will be waiting for him when he gets there. The medication will cure his problem quickly and, to his delight, with no unpleasant side effects.

There is no line at the exit window, and the cheerful secretary waives the co-pay. When the patient gets back to his car, it has been washed and simonized.

(They can't always get what they want, but if we try all the time, they just might find they get what they need.[*])

In July 1982, I joined the practice where I proceeded to work for almost thirty-five years. The three partners who hired me were all named Cohen—David Cohen, Michael Cohen, and Barry Cohen. They were

---

[*] After Jagger, M. and Richards, K.

not related. It was pure coincidence that each new partner who joined the practice happened to have been named Cohen. The house staff at our teaching hospital called them the Cohenheads.*

There was, of course, some initial patient resistance to seeing me, the new kid on the block. Patients would call for an appointment and say, "I'll see anyone named Cohen." The secretary would explain, "Dr. David, Dr. Michael and Dr. Barry are booked, but Dr. Baker can see you." The very next questions from the patient would almost invariably be, "Is he good? Is he nice?"

"Is he good?" I sort of get, though I wondered if patients thought that my partners would hire a *schlepper*. But, "Is he nice?" An unusual question to ask, no? But then the Cohens had a reputation of being exceedingly nice, and the patients wanted to know if they'd have the same good experience with the new guy.

As time went by and I interacted with more and more of my partners' patients, I noted something that I had never encountered with all the internists and specialists I had trained with over the years. Many patients regarded one of the doctors in our practice as not just their doctor, but also as their friend. I'd get a weekend phone call when I was on call for the practice, and the patient would say, "You don't know me yet, but I'm a friend of Dr. David and I need…"

One Monday morning I told David that his friend so-and-so had called, and he said, "Oh, he's not my friend, he's my patient."

"Well," I responded, "he seems to think he's your friend."

And David said, "I want all of my patients to feel I'm their friend." And suddenly I understood why he had one of the largest practices on the North Shore of Long Island.

Osler's second *A*: affability.

In my practice, I didn't want all the patients to think of me as their friend, but rather as their hired caring adviser. But I still treated them as if they were my friends—with warmth, courtesy, and respect. We

---

* If this reference is obscure to you, you are insufficiently informed about classic *Saturday Night Live*. Ask your parental units.

listen to our friends; we let them finish when they have something important to say; we're generous with our time with them.

Not surprisingly, these attributes of friendship are what patients *expect* from their doctors. When I was researching this book, I thought that there would be many different things that patients want from us. Yet, study after study concluded it was the same few items.

Aside from the given that patients expect us to be medically accurate in our diagnoses and correct in our treatments, what patients want from us falls under the broad rubric of "good bedside manner." Frankly, this is a term I dislike since we rarely visit patients at the bedside outside of hospital rounds and it's vague and all-encompassing. But we don't need to define it further, because in one way "good bedside manner" is like hard-core pornography. To quote Supreme Court Justice Potter Stewart in *Jacobellis v. Ohio*: "I know it when I see it."

Patients know it when doctors don't have it. In a 2013 study conducted by Vanguard Communications, 43.1 percent of the 3617 online reviews of three hundred practitioners contained complaints about the doctor's bedside manner. Most commonly cited failings were arrogance, indifference, and poor listening skills.[1]

If you ask patients what they want from their doctors, they'll tell you:

- They want us to listen to them.
- They want us to respect them.
- They want us to know them.
- They want us to give them enough time.

These wishes seem simple and, from the patients' point of view, entirely reasonable. But in the midst of a busy, tiring, hassled, overbooked day, they can be daunting, and even annoying, to us. You might be thinking:

- Of course I listen to patients; it's how I get their history. But there is a lot of information to collect in the short time allotted to a patient appointment, so sometimes I need to interrupt the patient, redirect him, or ask questions.

- I do respect my patients, but the fact is I have more medical knowledge than they do and the Internet research they want to tell me about rarely contributes to solving diagnostic and therapeutic problems, especially because patients are so susceptible to the Barnum Effect.*
- I simply cannot remember the medical details of the thousands of patients I see.
- I give every patient the amount of time he or she needs. But they always complain that all the time they had with me was "five minutes."

So a major goal of this book is to give patients a satisfying experience without burdening the doctor with extra things to do or requiring more time spent with patients.

A FACEBOOK SURVEY? REALLY?

PLEASE DON'T SCOFF. I DON'T have the money to fund a multicenter study of patient expectations of doctors. But I have several hundred "friends" on Facebook who were more than willing to share with me what they wanted from their doctors. There is plenty of ethnic and age diversity in that group.† So I set up a survey, and the results were qualitatively similar to those of more formal research studies.

In response to the open question, "What characteristics do you look for in a physician?" 40 percent used some form of the word *listen*. That result far exceeded answers like "competence" and "promptness."

---

* A type of subjective validation in which a person finds personal meaning in statements that could apply to many people, as in: "That website described all my symptoms exactly."

† But they may not represent an accurate cross section of the population of the United States of America.

Here's a sampling of their answers:

- "I want to feel he/she is REALLY [sic] listening to my concerns and not eyeballing the clock."
- "asking good questions, listening & understanding replies"
- "good listener, empathy, caring"
- "someone who listens and is kind; someone who doesn't rush you out and answers your questions"
- "someone who listens to complaints"
- "one who spends time with patient and truly listens"
- "compassion, empathy, great listening skills, humor"
- "somebody that really listens to what I'm saying, asks lots of questions"
- "listens to what I say—lets me finish a sentence"
- "good listener, responsive to my questions and concerns"
- "obvious that the doctor is listening to what I'm saying"
- "someone who actually listens"

We physicians have a reputation for not listening to our patients, for having our own agenda with our questions. This impression is reinforced by the finding that doctors tend to interrupt patients within twelve to eighteen seconds after they start speaking.[2] From our point of view, it almost makes sense: We're asking relevant questions as we drive toward a diagnosis. We have limited time to do this, so we need to cut to the proverbial chase.

Then there is the issue of the damned electronic health record and how it interferes with our listening. I believe that the EHR has become the biggest barrier between us and our patients, and I will offer ways to mitigate that interference.

I experienced resistance to using a computer as early as 1995. In that year, I first started taking notes on an early Apple laptop.* One impetus

---

* Being a committed early adopter, I had been searching for an excuse to buy one. Aha!—taking notes in the office!

for this was my poor handwriting, which has been lousy since I learned cursive in third grade. However, when patients commented that they could not read what I wrote, I explained that when I arrived in medical school I was observed to have excellent handwriting. The school forced me to take Chicken Scratch 101 to make my notes more doctor-like.

In truth, because of my bad handwriting, I always thought that the most valuable class I'd had in all my twenty-five years of schooling was typing in seventh grade. It had proved much more useful than, say, English constitutional history or organic chemistry.

On my office laptop, I templated my routine office visits, yearly physicals, and procedures so I could just type in the individual details for each patient. Then one day one of my partners told me that a patient had complained that "Dr. Baker just buried his face in the computer and didn't even look at me." That was a shocker. I really thought that I was good at listening and typing at the same time. So I vowed not to look at the computer at all as I talked to patients. My notes suffered, but my patient engagement improved. I actually started getting compliments from patients on how I could listen to them intently and type at the same time.

Aside from meeting our patients' needs and desires, we obviously have to be good at listening for the sake of our diagnostic acumen. As one of my teachers in residency taught, when making our diagnosis, 70 percent of the information comes from the history, 20 percent from our physical exam, and 10 percent from the tests (though patients think the exact opposite is true). Osler* said, "Listen to your patient, he is telling you the diagnosis."[3]

Patients are excellent at discerning if we're not really listening, and, by the way, The Powers That Be want to know if we're listening. Question 16 on the CAHPS survey asks, "…how often did your personal doctor listen carefully to you?" The answer'd better be "ALWAYS," so I'll discuss several ways to show patients that we really are listening.

---

* Him again!

R.E.S.P.E.C.T.

WE LIVE IN AN AGE when respect for expertise is on the decline. The reasons for this are many—political, sociological, devolutionary—and I have no interest in stirring more controversy than the basic tenet of this book already will. The availability of all the world's knowledge—including medical knowledge—in the palms of our hands can make anyone believe he's an instant expert. Further, the decentralization of medical care and the long overdue empowerment and participation of patients in their own care make doctors' need to respect patients and their opinions greater than ever.

Patients increasingly want to be involved in medical decisions. Early in my practice, when I'd ask patients what they thought of a diagnostic or therapeutic plan, they'd often demur, saying, "You're the doctor," or, "Whatever you say, Doc." Not so much anymore.

My policy with patients has long been that I'm their expert advisor. They've hired me for my knowledge, experience, and judgment, but they're the boss of their own health. I'm there to help. Does this sometimes lead to longer discussions than I'd like? To someone challenging my advice? Sure. But it more often than not creates a respectful partnership with the patient in which we're working toward the same goals.

There are many reasons patients believe that we are failing to respect them that we don't even realize. For instance, patients will often complain that doctors are "dismissive" of their concerns.[4] A patient coming in with a cough might express concern that he has pneumonia. We say, "No, I don't think so," and leave it at that. However, our failure to directly address that concern and the anxiety underlying it does not help the patient. After all, one can't counter emotions with facts, so if we nonchalantly or hurriedly try to do so, we debase the patient's emotions and thereby disrespect him.

Patients feel a lack of regard when we talk over their heads using medical jargon or below their dignity, dismissing their medical opinions.

Both of these behaviors are natural and understandable—to us. After all, our argot is so much a part of our daily lives that we don't even think about it. And the seven or more years of medical training we have would seem to bestow the right of at least a little medical arrogance. Our patients beg to disagree.

Any appearance of our being rushed also conveys disrespect to the patients. After all, they probably waited longer than they wanted to get an appointment or to see us once they arrived at the office or clinic, so they expect, rightfully, that we will give them enough of our time to justify the investment of theirs. Even if we *consciously* desire to give our patients adequate time with us, our manner and body language may *unconsciously* signal otherwise. When we address body language, I'll tell you about a really nifty way to give the patient the impression that you're spending more time with her without actually doing so.*

Other ways we can show disrespect to our patients include how we address them, how we undress them, and how we redress their grievances. To start, there is an immediate imbalance, an establishing of differential status, if my patient calls me Dr. Baker and I call him John.† The debates on how doctors and patients should address each other are legion and easily quelled—ask the patient what she prefers. More about that later.

The medical examination is frequently an invasive experience for the patient no matter how respectful and gentle we try to be. Of course, patients' expectations and behaviors vary. I have Orthodox Jewish women patients who have refused to greet me with a handshake, much less remove any clothing for an exam, which obliged me to work around what they were wearing. And men's reactions to impending prostate examinations have run the gamut from dread to dread.

Then there was the twenty-something-year-old French mistress of one of my middle-aged-plus patients whom he brought to me for a

---

* Did I just write "nifty," or only think it?
† Especially if that's not his name, which (sigh) I've done.

pelvic examination. During the exam, she casually leafed through a copy of *Paris Match*. Then, when the exam was over, I told her she could get dressed. Before I could get out of the room, she hopped off the exam table, nonchalantly let her exam gown drop to the floor, and started to retrieve her clothes. I quickly left the room, shall we say—flustered?

One of the most important, and consequential, ways we can disrespect patients is in how we handle their complaints. Often, a feeling of having been treated without respect can trigger a lawsuit that might otherwise have been prevented. That's the worst-case scenario, but an unhappy patient could simply leave the practice, which can cause a ripple of consequences.

A 1999 study by the Institute of Quality showed that about 50 percent of patients who had a complaint about a doctor's office would not mention it to the practice. But 97 percent of those patients *told at least ten other people* about their bad experience. These days, dissatisfied patients can post online and tell seven billion people about it. In Chapter 11, When Things Go Wrong, we'll see ways physicians have satisfied patients who have complaints as well as ways they, and I, have not.

FAMILIARITY BREEDS CONTENTEDNESS

WE'VE ALL HEARD DOCTORS' OFFICES and clinics disparagingly referred to as "factories" and "assembly lines." As the amount of time physicians have to devote to patient visits has shrunk, as technology has continued its relentless push into the office, and as changing insurance plans have forced patients to change from doctor to doctor, medicine has come to feel increasingly impersonal.

This is indeed unfortunate, since the doctor-patient relationship is such a crucial component of healing. As By-Now-You-Can-Guess-Who said, "It is much more important to know what sort of a patient has a disease than what sort of a disease a patient has."[5]

Further, our patients trust us with their most valuable possession—their health—and they have the right to expect that we know them as individuals and not just as another body coming through the door.

The first thing that a review of 900 HCAHPS surveys and 124 patient and family interviews revealed to researchers at the Cleveland Clinic was that "patients want more respect," meaning that "they want to be recognized as an individual, not as a patient."[6]

Of course, with thousands of patients in our practices, it's impossible to remember the names, much less the medical histories of all of them, though some seem to think we can. I swear to you that I was eating dinner with my parents in a restaurant in Boca Raton, Florida, when a woman came up to me and asked me how her cholesterol results, taken a few days earlier, had come back. My first thought was, "Are you kidding me? I don't even know who the hell you are!"

Would that we all had the memories of King Cyrus the Great of Persia who, according to Pliny the Younger, knew the name of every soldier in his army. Or Scipio, who knew the name of every citizen of Rome. Of course, those guys were not expected to keep soldiers' and citizens' lab data in their heads.

If you're more like me in the memory department, you'll like using the techniques in Chapter 6 to show patients that you do know them.

TEMPUS FUGIT... AND QUICKLY

FINALLY, PATIENTS WANT US TO give them enough time. It seems that many have come to the conclusion that the average doctor visit is "five minutes." As in, "I waited an hour to see him, and he was in and out in five minutes." This perception can have direct consequences on our patient ratings, as Question 18 of the CAHPS asks, "…how often did your personal doctor spend enough time with you?"

Sometimes, the perception is not far from the truth. One practice I know allots 7.5 minutes to each patient visit. Blood pressure check? 7.5 minutes. FUO? 7.5 minutes. Family discussion of a new cancer diagnosis and options for treatment? All right, give them two 7.5-minute time slots.

More realistically, a 2007 study found the average length of a visit for elderly patients using practices in the southwest United States was 15.7 minutes.[7] I strongly suspect the time is less now. The authors point out, "In clinical practice today, it appears, visit lengths may be prescribed by physicians' practice settings. Physicians are often held to daily patient volume targets that can also limit the amount of time they spend with patients." Daily patient volume targets? Journal-speak for productivity demands.

So doctors and patients are at loggerheads. Patients want more time with us, and we have less to give. Fortunately, there is a near-magical way to ameliorate this problem. You guessed it: We're getting there soon.

DON'T WORRY; BE HAPPY.

THERE'S ONE MORE THING PATIENTS want that I found interesting: They want us to enjoy our work. In my Facebook survey, 93.5 percent of responders considered it important or very important that their physicians enjoyed their work. The Cleveland Clinic researchers discovered the same thing, and found this to be "one of the most baffling findings."[8] But Dr. Merlino concluded that patient perception of providers' happiness is actually about how physicians comport themselves in front of patients, what attitude they bring into the examination room.

For me, this is one more reason why it's valid to treat every patient visit as a performance. Doing so enables us to walk in with a fresh, positive attitude for each patient we see. Every one of them is, after all, a new audience.

To give our patients better experiences, we must be ever-mindful of their desires—that we listen to them, that we respect them, that we know them, and that we give them enough time. Even though patients' wants may not be expressly spoken during a visit, our failure to satisfy them by our actions and attitudes will leave patients with the feeling that something vital was missing in the visit. In the next chapter, we'll discuss practical performance techniques that will ensure that our patients never feel that way.

TAKEAWAYS

- Patients want us to listen to them.
- They want us to respect them.
- They want us to know them.
- They want us to give them enough time.

SECTION II
TECHNIQUES AND STRATEGIES

CHAPTER 5
THE FIVE BASIC PERFORMANCE TECHNIQUES WE NEED

THEORIES OF ACTING CAN BE neatly summarized by a famous, partially apocryphal story of an interaction between Dustin Hoffman and Sir Laurence Olivier on the set of the 1976 movie *Marathon Man*. To prepare for a scene in which Hoffman's character had stayed up for seventy-two hours and looked it, Hoffman told Olivier that he actually had not slept for seventy-two hours straight to achieve the greatest possible realism. Responded Olivier, in his mellifluous voice, "Why don't you try acting?"[1]

Hoffman was "method" acting, doing what actors refer to as "acting from within," living his character's life, calling on his own emotions and experiences to inform his character's. This technique, originated by Konstantin Stanislavski, was preached in America by Lee Strasberg, Sanford Meisner, and Stella Adler at the Group Theater and had acolytes such as Hoffman and Marlon Brando.

Olivier was "acting from the outside in." He assumed the walk, the mannerisms, the speech of the Nazi war criminal-dentist he was portraying and thereby became him on the screen. Clearly, Sir Laurence's technique worked, as he created one of the great film villains of all time and won an Academy Award nomination for Best Supporting Actor.

To create great performances for our patients, we'll take the Olivier approach. This is because we are layering practical acting techniques on top of our authentic behavior to create a better experience for both patients and us. No need to call on "emotion memory," as Stanislavski called it.[2] To effectively work with a patient with cancer, for instance, we do not need to call up the emotions we might have had when a close relative had cancer.

The five techniques we'll employ are:

1. Listening and Observing
2. Responding in the Moment
3. Staying in Character
4. Acting as if…
5. Breathing

LISTENING AND OBSERVING

Acting is just listening, so if you're really there with a person, you're picking up what they're about.
—*Meryl Streep*[3]

You just hold the eyes of the other person and listen. And listening is really what acting is all about for movies.
—*Michael Caine*[4]

Listening, true listening, requires more than our ears. It also requires paying attention to the patient's facial expressions and, to a lesser degree, body language.

I'm not a subscriber to the meme that 93 percent of interpersonal communication is nonverbal, that is, 58 percent comes from facial expression, 38 percent from voice, and only 7 percent from words.[5] Nor do I believe the claim that nonverbal communication is 12.5 times as powerful as words in interpersonal communication.[6] The studies supporting these assertions are deeply flawed, primarily because they did not study actual real-world communication, but rather lab simulacra. In addition, the participants knew that the studies were researching body language's role in communication. In other research, when the purpose of the study was unknown to the participants, the body language predominance could not be reproduced.[7]

However, even though the role of nonverbal communication is less than is often claimed, that doesn't mean it's nonexistent. If we are hunched over our computers or tablets while patients are speaking, we can easily miss emotions that underlie their words. Conversely, as we'll see in Chapter 7, our body language sends patients a message when we're concentrating on our EHR device.

Seven basic human emotions can be recognized by universal facial expressions: joy, surprise, contempt, sadness, anger, disgust, and fear. They are "universal" because they are recognized cross-culturally around the world.[8] Even people blind since birth, who have never seen a human face, use the same facial expressions to show emotions when they speak.

In addition to the more obvious facial expressions, we all unconsciously use so-called microexpressions. These are fleeting (taking as little as 1/30 of a second) changes in facial expression that reflect concealed emotions. Microexpressions are very hard to recognize consciously without training. To find out how hard, try this online test: http://www.centerforbodylanguage.com/micro-expressions-test/.[9] I scored a whopping 2 percent correct.

I'm not suggesting that training in microexpression recognition or body language training is a necessity for physicians, though it couldn't hurt.[10] But we need to both listen to our patients' words *and* observe the patients so as not to miss nuances of what they're telling us.

By "observing," I don't mean simply seeing them. "Observing" means being consciously aware of what we see, and it's very possible to see things without observing them, especially if we approach the patient with presumptions about him. I had a dramatic example of that in my practice.

I have a patient I'll call Mr. Anderson, who is a middle school teacher. He's a large man with a belly like Santa Claus's, a big, booming voice, and an even bigger personality. You just know when you meet him that he's one of those teachers all the kids love.

One day Mr. A. came to see me with a fever and a cough. On exam, he had râles in his chest, so I suggested that we take an X-ray to rule out pneumonia. Our X-ray machine is right in the office, so I invited him to walk up the hall with me to take the pictures.

Imagine this very large man sitting shirtless on the small exam table. He asks me, "Doc, should I put on a gown first?" I was running a bit behind in my schedule, so I replied, "No, it's just a short walk up the hall. Pretend you're at the beach."

Mr. Anderson didn't object—aloud—but I saw a brief look of apprehension flash across his face—a microexpression. In retrospect, I realize that I *saw* it, but I didn't *observe* it and so didn't act on it.

We took the X-ray, it showed an RLL pneumonia, and I treated him. Soon he was recovered and back to teaching. End of story, right? Wrong. Mr. Anderson decided to post online about his visit. Did he praise me for correctly diagnosing and treating his pneumonia? Nope. He wrote, "When *they* [meaning *me*] take you for an X-ray, they make you walk through the halls half naked."

Good patient outcome. Bad patient experience. Result: mediocre doctor rating.

The problem was that I had *assumed* that, because he was a man, Mr. Anderson wouldn't mind walking through the hall without his shirt. And in making that assumption, I missed his subtle objection and didn't act on it. And really, it probably would have delayed me perhaps another 12.23 seconds in my busy day if I'd simply given him a gown.

So, technique number one is listening to the patient and observing what is really going on.

RESPONDING IN THE MOMENT

BEING "IN THE MOMENT" GOES by other names, including being fully present and being mindful. It's a concept that derives from Zen

Buddhism, and I like the definition given by Bodhipaksa, a member of the Buddhist Triratna order: "...being in the moment means being mindfully aware of what is going on right here and now, in our experience..."[11]

For actors, Scottish acting coach Mark Westbrook writes, "...being 'in the moment' means being present. Not present, like physically attending, but a developed sense of the self and others in the exact and precise here and now. When you're an actor, it's very difficult to 'be in the moment' because the future has so much meaning. The future movement you need to make, the future objective to be achieved, the future line you have to deliver."[12]

For physicians, the future has "much meaning" too. While seeing the patient, we are often thinking ahead: to the plan developing in our minds for this patient, to the patients waiting to see us, to the return phone call we're expecting from a colleague, to dinner, to the soccer game we have to coach. Thoughts about work and life responsibilities have a way of intruding, and it takes active concentration to shut them out and be fully present for the patient we are with.

When we let our minds wander, we are not serving our patients well; we are also not serving ourselves well. Matthew A. Killingsworth and Daniel T. Gilbert from the University of California at San Francisco have studied the relationship between happiness and mind-wandering in over fifteen thousand people from around the world.[13] They found that when people focused on what they were doing, they were much happier than when their minds wandered from the activity they were doing, no matter what or how enjoyable that particular activity was.[14]

So even if we are seeing a patient we don't much like (and I know you *do* have some), if we stay focused on the patient—remain in the moment—we will feel better about it than if we let our minds wander, even to think about something pleasant. This may explain why, when we're really "into" our work, we enjoy it more, and the day goes by faster.

Another problem with staying in the moment is that so much of what we do is repetitive. We ask a lot of the same questions, do the same basic physical examination, look at the same lab data. It's easy, when seeing the third URI of the day, for instance, to go on autopilot. I know there have been times when performing a routine "well-baby" physical my thoughts have wandered and suddenly I'll ask myself, "How were the heart sounds, or the abdominal exam?"

Theater actors have the same issue, performing the same play night after night after night. They, too, can go on autopilot and thereby ruin a scene. Perhaps they miss a change that another actor makes to a line or they lose their place in the script. Indeed, thinking ahead can make an actor forget lines. So they train themselves to remain in the moment.

They must remember that every night it's a new audience who've never seen the play. Similarly, we must remember that every time we enter the exam room, even if we know the patient well, this visit is a new experience for her and a new performance for us. It's a new audience every time we walk into the room. On this account, I take inspiration from the great Yankees center fielder Joe DiMaggio who, when asked why he played so hard every day, responded, "There is always some kid who may be seeing me for the first or last time, I owe him my best."[15] You know, when he was playing, he was always in the moment so he could respond immediately to any ball hit or pitch thrown to him.

We need consciously to be in the moment, too, so we take in everything the patient is telling us and thereby can *respond* appropriately to what the patient is saying. This is not the same as *reacting* to the patient. Reacting is a reflex and responding is a choice, so our initial *reaction* may not be the *response* that the patient needs.

For instance, if a patient tells me that he's gone on the Internet and, on the basis of his research, has decided to stop taking his statin, my internal *reaction* might be something along the lines of, "Are you crazy? You're a forty-five-year-old diabetic hypertensive smoker with a family history of coronary artery disease, and you're getting your medical advice from Dr. Google?"

Even though reprimanding patients might be our first impulse, we've all learned, often the hard way, that it's counterproductive to gaining their compliance. So our *response* to bad medical behavior needs to be modulated. In this case, I'd ask the patient to explain what he'd learned, discuss that rationally and respectfully, and then offer my reasons for having recommended the statin in the first place. To respond appropriately, we need to be fully present with the patient and to be sure we are...

STAYING IN CHARACTER

Be yourself. Everyone else is already taken.
*—Oscar Wilde**

Becoming a magician, which I've been for fifty years, is a daunting task. It requires years of study of classic and modern texts and journals, countless hours of practice to master certain skills, and a lifelong commitment to continuous learning. Sound familiar, doctor?

One piece of advice frequently given to young magicians who wonder how they should present themselves onstage is to "be yourself." In one way, that makes sense. It's more than a little silly when a pimply thirteen-year-old stands onstage with a box painted with Chinese characters and claims to be a traveler to "the Mysterious Far East."†

On the other hand, the advice to "be yourself" onstage is useless because "yourself" is usually not very interesting to an audience. Performers need to be bigger, better versions of "themselves" on stage.

I keep putting "yourself" in quotation marks because there is no single self. We all have many selves depending on the circumstances we are in, the people we are with, and the impression we are trying to

---

* Reportedly.
† Been there, done that.

create. We contain our physician selves, our managing partner selves, our parent selves, our spouse selves, our kids' basketball coach selves, and on and on.

As I mentioned in Chapter 2, Erving Goffman thoroughly explored this concept in his seminal work *The Presentation of Self in Everyday Life*.[16] He defines performance as "all the activity of a given participant on a given occasion which serves to influence in any way any of the other participants." Kind of sounds like a doctor's visit, doesn't it?

When we are with patients we should be the biggest, best version of our *physician* selves. That is the character we are playing, the character we must stay in.

Goffman says these life performances occur on a spectrum, with the extremes being "sincere" or "cynical."[17,*] In the former case, both the performer and the audience believe that "the reality which he stages is the real reality." In the latter case, "the performer may be moved to guide the conviction of his audience as a means to an end." For instance, helping them to achieve better health.

As is always the case with spectra, most people fall somewhere in the middle and frequently will oscillate along the spectrum. What you will find with the techniques and strategies I present here is that what may start off seeming manipulative or "cynical," with practice becomes sincere and magnifies your doctor self.

One way to stay in character is to be consciously aware that you are doing so. That way, every minute you are in the exam room with the patient you are being your best doctor self, regardless of what is going on outside that room—in the office, the hospital, your private life. Just as the actor onstage loses herself in her character, we must completely become our doctor selves when we are "onstage" with our patients.

But really, how do we do that? By staying in the moment and listening to the patient. As acting coach Dr. Charles Northrup says, "To listen in character is one of the most important secrets to successful

---

[*] Goffman wasn't thinking in terms of a physician helping a patient, so in our domain, "cynical" might not be the most accurate descriptor.

acting."[18] In addition, British acting teacher Ruth Kulerman advises, "Pay attention to what is happening on stage. Don't let your mind wander and be distracted... Stay in the moment and stay connected to your scene."[19]

In other words, to be your best physician self with every patient, stay in the moment, listen and observe. But we're all human. Even with our best efforts, outside influences can make us break character. Even a lousy day can do that, and it can be hard to find our way back to our best physician selves. Some days we have to...

ACTING AS IF

SIMPLY PUT, THIS MEANS THAT if we act in a certain way, we will feel it and then become it.

For example, when we're happy, we smile, but if we smile it makes us feel happy.[20] If we're alert, awake, and feeling good, we have good posture. Conversely, if we assume good posture, it makes us feel better and more alert.[21] So please, if you're slumping while reading this, kindly sit up.

Examples of the power of "acting as if" abound. In literature, think of the poor flower girl Eliza Doolittle in George Bernard Shaw's *Pygmalion*. (Or Lerner and Loewe's *My Fair Lady*, if you're musically inclined.) Henry Higgins teaches her to act as if she were a lady. She does so well enough to fool even Zoltan Karpathy, whom Higgins calls "that hairy hound from Budapest."* By the end of the play, we know that Eliza has indeed become a lady.

In real life, soldiers are trained to act courageously so that in battle they can truly be brave.

For actors, acting as if creates the reality of their characters. When an actress acts as if another actor is her husband, she can become the

---

* "Never have I ever seen a ruder pest." (Great rhymes deserve repetition regardless of context.)

character of the wife, and all her lines and actions in relation to him will be performed as that character.

A popular adage is "fake it 'til you make it." I prefer what Harvard social psychologist Amy Cuddy says in her [in]famous TED talk: "Fake it until you become it."[22]

If all this sounds too showbiz for you, I like what Jerry Sternin, the founder of Save the Children, said. "It's easier to act your way into a new way of thinking than to think your way into a new way of acting."[23]

If you act as your best doctor self in every way, you will be your best doctor self. I'm not suggesting that we must consciously act as if with patients, but rather that we simply need to be constantly aware of which self we are putting forward to our patients and be the best version of ourselves we can be—no matter how stressed we are, no matter what's going on in our private lives, no matter how we feel that day.

Acting as if can have powerful physiological effects.

When I was in medical school, I was friendly with a younger magician from New Jersey named David Kotkin. We would hang out in the back of magicians' society meetings and snicker at the old "magicians." David was, at the time, debating whether he should go to college or become a full-time magician. I told him that it was really hard to have a career in show business and that he needed a college education to fall back on in case the showbiz thing didn't work out.

As you may have guessed, I went on to spend my life sticking tubes into people, and he went on to become David Copperfield. But he told me a story that demonstrates the power of acting as if.

When he was only nineteen years old, David was cast to play the lead in a musical called *The Magic Man* in Chicago. In fact, he dropped out of New York University after only two weeks there to star in the play. Fool.

On opening night, about an hour before curtain, David came down with the flu. He had a fever over 103, chills, myalgias, and a terrible headache. There was no understudy. David was the show. He had to go on. How did he do it? He acted as if he felt well. That night he gave a performance that won rave reviews and launched his career. And he told me that, for those two hours onstage, he didn't feel ill.*

You may recall that I opened Chapter 2 with the story of my patient whose daughter had lissencephaly and had just come home from the hospital for the last time. It was an emotionally devastating visit for me, and yet I had an obligation to perform at the top of my game for the next patient, who was having a routine physical exam.

How did I do it? By acting as if. As if I had the strength to get through the physical. As if making up the twenty-five minutes that I was then running behind was extremely important to me. As if there was no place in the world I wanted to be more than in that room with that patient.

By acting it, I felt it and did it. And I was able to be the best version of my physician self for that patient.

I'm certain that every person who reads this book has had a similar experience, where something extremely upsetting occurs in the office or the hospital and yet we have to carry on with our obligations. After all, the subsequent patients don't know what is going on outside their own exam room and they don't care. What they want is for us to be at our best for them, and that's when we need to be able to act as if.

BREATHING

I KNOW. I KNOW. I know. You already know how to breathe. You have, after all, been doing it pretty much all your life. Or at least your medulla has been getting your diaphragm to do the work for you. So what do actors mean when they talk about the importance of breathing?

There are two things. First, there are the breathing techniques necessary to produce a good sound, one that can project to the farthest reaches of a theater. These techniques combine oral, diaphragmatic,

---

* If you should run into David somewhere, don't bother giving him my regards. I saw him at a show a few years ago; he pretended to remember me, kind of like how I've had to pretend to remember patients I saw outside the office.

and mental skills to shape the sound and quality of the actor's voice. They are crucial to acting, but not really our concern here.

But there is another aspect of breathing that actors use to help them communicate better with their audiences. I learned about it from my vocal coach, Scott Miller, who is an associate arts professor at the NYU Tisch School of the Arts in their revered Graduate Acting Program *and* a former professional baseball and basketball player *and* a law school graduate. I like him anyway.

Scott is interested in how our breathing affects what we communicate with other people. Notice I said *with* other people, not *to* other people, because the communication between a performer and the audience is a two-way street, just as it is between a physician and a patient. Scott notes that how a doctor breathes when seeing a patient can signal either openness or unavailability that a patient registers unconsciously.

Scott says, "If the doctor is completely staccato with his voice, is holding his breath a lot, is closing his mouth a lot, is looking around the room and not making eye contact, all those things tend to be distractions because the unconscious mind of the patient is actually taking all that information in and having to make some decisions about that." The patient is getting a "feel" for the doctor.

While it's readily understandable how to get the "feel" of a single person, what about a whole room full of people? Performers learn from experience how to gauge the atmosphere, the ambience, that a group of people—an audience—gives off. A seasoned performer can walk onstage and sense a friendly or hostile audience before he says a word. You've almost certainly experienced something similar. Even if you have no performing experience, you've probably gotten the "feel" of a room, say at a party you were attending or conference you went to. Call it the "feel" or the "vibe," you sense it, but would probably be hard-pressed to explain it.

How do we make that assessment? It happens unconsciously and almost instantaneously. Our brains are gathering vast amounts of information at every moment, and by looking at " 'thin slices' of the information, we extract just what we need for making quick judgments."[24] Our ability to do so and the remarkable frequency with which we arrive at correct conclusions are the subjects of Malcom Gladwell's fascinating book *Blink: The Power of Thinking Without Thinking.*[25]

So, if a performer encounters a friendly room, she senses it and is off and running. A good opening interaction with the audience and she's "got them," because they are making "thin slice" judgments about her, too. If the room seems hostile or, worse, indifferent, she needs to change that dynamic and win the audience over. And the way she does it is by being open, almost vulnerable, to the audience.

It seems paradoxical, to be vulnerable before a hostile audience. But communicating vulnerability is a way to communicate humanity, to communicate openness to other humans, and even indifferent or hostile audiences can warm to that.

And that's where doctoring comes in. One of the most important things we can do is to communicate our humanity to our patients. Letting them see our humanity opens them to communication, and that's the first step to healing.

When a performer has connected with an audience, they both actually breathe together. This phenomenon is well known among actors. Unconsciously, audience members start to breathe in sync with the performer; their inhalations and exhalations mirror his. Therefore, well-trained performers keep their breath moving, one breath following the other without a pause after inhalation or exhalation, giving the audience a model they will unconsciously mirror.

Try this: As you sit reading, take note of how you are breathing. Are you breathing through your nose or your mouth? At the end of each inhalation, is there a brief pause before you exhale, a momentary holding of your breath? After you exhale, is there short pause before you start your next inhalation?

Now try this technique: Breathe gently through your mouth and go directly into the next phase of the breathing cycle as soon as one finishes. In other words, the instant you reach the top of your inhalation, start to allow the air out through your open mouth. Then, the very moment the last bit of air is out, start your next inhalation, again with your mouth open. Don't close your mouth between breaths; keep it open. Not wide open, just lips parted. Repeat with every breath.

This is not rapid or forced breathing. Exhale simply by allowing your chest/abdomen/diaphragm to relax, allowing the air to escape through your mouth. Then immediately start the next inhalation at the bottom of that breath. It is not a deep or rapid inhalation. Don't take a full, deep breath. Just inhale easily and almost effortlessly. As soon as you reach the top of the breath, which is *not* maximum inhalation, just let it ease out by relaxing the abdominal muscles/diaphragm.

At first, this will feel a bit strange and unnatural, but it quickly becomes easy. This is how stage actors and singers learn to breathe when performing, and it's how we should breathe when seeing patients.

To understand why, try this little experiment. Next time you're in conversation with someone, try breathing in the gentle, cyclical manner I described, keeping your mouth slightly open to breathe through it. Then, abruptly close your mouth and breathe only through your nose, allowing the little pauses between inhalations and exhalations to happen.

Pay close attention to how the other person is responding to you after you make the switch. Do you note a subtle difference, a change in the amount of information that is being transmitted back and forth? By closing your mouth as you listen, you signal that you are closing yourself off to the information that the other person is sending you.

In my public speaking I have noticed that audience responses are much better since I started applying Scott's techniques in my speeches. More germane to our purposes, I also started breathing "Scott's way" when seeing patients. I noticed that conversations felt more relaxed for both me and the patients. They communicated more freely, and I even noticed that some started to mirror my breathing pattern, demonstrating a clear, if unconscious, connection.

I realize this breathing technique will strike at least some of you as a bit woo-woo. Not terribly scientific. Unsupported by randomized, double-blind trials. Unappealing to your rational brain. I get that. But the Oscar-, Tony-, and Emmy-winning actors Scott Miller coaches use his technique. You just might like it too.

ACTING TECHNIQUES AND EMPATHY

THIS IS THE CRUX OF bringing acting techniques into the exam room. Simply by consciously listening and observing, responding in the moment, staying in character, acting as if, and breathing openly, we actually become what we are trying to be—more present, more responsive, more empathic, happier physicians. We are "acting our way into a new way of thinking" and, indeed, a new way of being. It happens by itself and it feels good.

TAKEAWAYS

- We are using performance techniques to enhance our authentic behavior.
- True listening requires attention to facial expressions and body language.
- Our assumptions about patients can affect our observations of them.
- Reacting is a reflex; responding is a choice.
- Being in the moment benefits both patients and us.
- Staying in the moment helps us stay in character—our doctor selves.
- Acting as if can get us through difficult days.
- Breathing cyclically with mouth slightly open makes us more relatable.
- Using all these techniques together enhances our empathy.

CHAPTER 6
SETTING THE STAGE: WHAT TO DO BEFORE YOU GO IN WITH THE PATIENT

As a house manager, patrons *often ask me, "When does the show begin?" I look at them matter-of-factly and reply, "Why... the show has already begun!" The reactions I get vary. Some glance at me with a puzzled look, while others resort to sheer panic. I then explain, "On paper, the show begins at eight p.m., but technically, the show began the second you pulled into our parking lot and met our valet attendant." After the rush of adrenaline wears off, the patron chuckles or issues a sigh of relief and walks in the direction of the theatre...*

If a patron makes it to their seat with smooth sailing, they will be in the right frame of mind to enjoy the show. If a patron experiences a bumpy road along the way, for example, a rude valet attendant, an un-knowledgeable box office representative, unsanitary facilities, or an usher that ignores them, they will be less likely to enjoy the show, which can affect the most important form of advertising...WORD OF MOUTH!

—Mike Abramson
When Does the Show Begin?[1]

Substitute the word "patient" for the word "patron," and you understand why the ideal patient experience starts long before he comes face to face with you. Everything and everyone the patient encounters affects his perception of the visit and thereby affects what he says to others or reports on a survey or online rating site. Indeed, I think the experience begins even earlier than Mr. Abramson, the theatre* house manager, suggests. I'd say it starts with the phone call the patient makes to get an appointment.

I certainly have no intention of telling you how to run your practice or clinic. There are full-time professionals and consultants to do that. Hospitals and large clinics even have CXOs, chief experience officers, whose *raison d'être* is customer service. There are people, like me, who hate hearing patients referred to as "customers." However, institutions and practices are competing for patients now, so we'd better think the way businesses do that try to please their customers.

Besides, the vast majority of complaints about doctors' offices are about "customer service." In a review of almost thirty-five thousand online patient reviews, Vanguard Communications found that 96 percent of patient complaints were about customer service issues, not about the physicians.[2]

Consequently, I'm sharing with you some simple suggestions and techniques that take virtually no extra time on your part or on the part of your staff but which will help ensure that your patients experience "smooth sailing" before seeing you.

THE VENUE

UNLESS WE OWN OUR OWN office building, we doctors don't have a lot of control over the patient experience before they get to the office itself. Several characteristics of the building register at least unconsciously with the patients, including convenience, decor, maintenance, and cleanliness.[3]

At one point, our practice was actually losing patients because the parking situation in our office's lot was so godawful. People would arrive

---

* Spelled thus because he's British.

late for appointments because they had been cruising the parking lot looking for spaces. My office window overlooked the parking lot, and I sometimes heard shouting and honking matches between patients competing for a spot. Finally, we got together with other practices in the building and persuaded (browbeat) the landlord into hiring a valet service.

Interestingly, when I asked patients if the parking situation had improved with the addition of the valet, most said yes even though they had not actually used him. I thought that strange and watched the valet out my office window. He didn't seem particularly efficient at moving cars. I suspect that the patients were more satisfied with the parking situation simply because they saw that *something* was being done about it.

Theaters often use the audience space, the "house," to create atmosphere for the play even before the curtain goes up. For the London hit *Ghost Stories* by Andy Nyman and Jeremy Dyson, the theater was decorated with strange symbols and had mysterious dripping sounds echoing over the sound system. Audiences were being primed to be scared.

When we walk into someone's house for the first time, we make an immediate judgment about the people who live there. If the house is neat and clean, it suggests that the residents care about their own appearance and cleanliness. Are the decor choices stark or welcoming? If there are toys and junk all over the place, we suspect the presence of toddlers or teenagers. Professor Sam Gosling of the University of Texas has devoted his life's research to what we are telling people about ourselves in our homes, offices, and other personal spaces and writes about it in his fun and fascinating book, *Snoop*.[4]

The decor of our "audience" space will affect how people perceive the practice and the practitioners. I've seen offices whose decor ranges from ultramodern (plastic surgeon) to functional (orthopedist), warm and fuzzy (psychiatrist) to madhouse (pediatrician). To the extent that you have control over your office's decor, consider what impression you want your patients to have the moment they walk in.

I know that I really shouldn't need to stress the importance of cleanliness in a doctor's office. However, we get so used to a situation as it is, we can miss how it might strike another person. Years ago, I read a story (and I can't find where or by whom) about leaving a broom in the corner. Someone was sweeping his living room when a friend came by to visit. He stopped sweeping, set the broom in a corner, and the two friends went out. One thing followed another, then one day followed another, and the broom remained where it was. Weeks later, another friend came to the house and asked him, "Why do you keep a broom in the corner?" The man replied, "What broom?"

So if our waiting room tends to get a little messy, with magazines and patients' Starbucks cups left lying around, we may not notice it. If the bathroom sink is not spotless, or if the toilet paper roll needs replacement, we might just leave it to a staff member to take care of. We're used to these deficiencies, but our patients are not. They expect a neat, clean, spotless office—with toilet paper. Why would we settle for anything less?

And one pet peeve I must get off my chest because I can do it here: old, grossly outdated, wrinkled, partially torn, coverless magazines tossed around the waiting room. These seem to be a universal affliction of medical offices. They show patients that we've made little effort to make their space pleasant and comfortable.

The solution is simple. Ask staff to bring in their magazines from home the moment they are finished with them. You might offer a free one-year renewal to the staff member who brings in the most magazines in good condition. Assign one staff member a week to keep the waiting room neat and replace and remove magazines. If all that is too hard to do, get rid of the magazines entirely. People have their phones to entertain them.

Thanks. I feel better.

SUPPORTING CAST

SOMETIMES SOMETHING A PARENT SAYS to us just sticks, and it can be hard to know why, of the many things they have told us, one stands out. Many years ago, my mother returned from a visit to her gynecologist complaining about how "nasty" the office's receptionist was. Mom said, "If the secretary is nasty, the doctor is nasty. He sets the tone for the office."

I think there's some truth there, even considering the source. In my experience, kind doctors tend to have kind office staff. The staff take their behavioral cues from "the boss." Further, the staff's attitude reflects how the doctors treat them. Kindness breeds kindness, and disrespect breeds disrespect.

It's so easy to become frustrated with staff and to forget that their "customer relations" job is harder than ours. They often have to deal with patients when they are at their worst: either they're sick or they think they are. It doesn't matter which. People who don't feel well become anxious, impatient, and easily frustrated when they feel a health situation is not being addressed quickly and efficiently. I'm sure that patients who have behaved monstrously to staff when trying to get an appointment would be perfectly lovely when chatting at a cocktail party. In fact, I've often been surprised when staff have complained to me about the behavior of patients who were models of courtesy and respect when seeing me, but who were rude and condescending with the office personnel.

Many resources are available to help with managing staff, and consultants can come in to advise improved procedures. Choose the latter carefully, though. In 1994, our practice hired an outside consulting firm for a ton of money to help us create a better workplace for our staff. We thought.

When we implemented their suggestions, some disgruntled office staff went to a local labor union and they, in turn, tried to unionize our office—that's right, a private medical practice. We actually had to have an election in our office. Imagine how pleasant it was to come to work every day feeling under attack from the staff and the union. In the end, the union lost by a single vote. Twenty-plus years later, and I still have a bitter taste in my mouth from the episode. So be careful whose advice you follow.

Fortunately, consultants today take a different approach, emphasizing the importance of good communications, respect, and empathy. But the real agenda has to be set by the doctors. Internist and author Danielle Ofri put it this way:

> Doctors have to take a good deal of the blame. For better or worse, we often set the tone in a medical enterprise. When we show, or tolerate, even subtle disrespect, it works its way all along the chain.
>
> Luckily, the reverse is true. Having had the privilege of working under some of the most humane and respectful doctors, I have witnessed how everyday acts of decency and humility generate positive cascading effects toward other staff members and toward patients. Rising tides, in this case, can indeed lift all boats.[5]

I think of it even more simply: How would I want my mother to be treated? If every doctor thought this way about staff and every staff member thought this way about patients, I suspect patient complaints about doctor's offices would approach zero.

Asymptotically, of course.

AUDIENCE MANAGEMENT: PATIENTS-IN-WAITING

In the Vanguard Communications study of patient complaints, 35 percent of the complaints were about waiting time. 53 percent were about poor communication. It seems clear, then, that the answer to patient frustration about waiting is in better communication.

For many reasons, it's damned near impossible for us physicians to run on time. Patients come late; they have fifteen-minute appointments and thirty-minute problems; we get interrupted with tasks that need our immediate attention; emergencies do occur; we poop out; we have to poop.

But guess what. Patients don't care. The best we can hope is that they will understand and accept the waiting if the situation is explained truthfully.

I think patients see through "the doctor had an emergency" or "she's delayed at the hospital," and they don't believe these common, mundane excuses, even when they're true. However, these seem like unassailable reasons for the delay, so the patient has no choice but to accept the reason, sit quietly, and wait. These rationales satisfy the staff, but not the patients.

Fortunately, there are better ways to mollify the pain of waiting. Research on waiting has revealed some factors that frustrate people waiting in line. Knowing these, we can mitigate them. Business consultant David Maister[6] outlines several, of which the following directly apply to physicians' offices:

- Unoccupied time feels longer than occupied time.
- People want to get started.
- Uncertain waits are longer than known, finite waits.
- Unexplained waits are longer than explained waits.

Let's take the first two together. Many practices have patients fill out multi-page questionnaires upon arrival. This occupies considerable time, and it's fine for first-timers to provide this information to the practice. For returning patients, however, these forms are a frustrating waste of time. When I have to fill them out, I feel that the time spent is delaying my appointment, not helping me pass the time productively.

I suggest that returning patients be given only two pieces of paper. One should be a list of their medications as recorded in EHR so that they can make any necessary updates. The second should be a lined sheet on which they are invited to record the three main issues or questions they want to cover in the day's visit. These simple tasks will occupy their time productively, help them "get started," and save the doctor from having to sit through a lot of uhhhhs, blank looks, and oh-by-the-ways in the exam room.

Fortunately, many patients bring time killers with them in the form of their phones, tablets, and computers. Hence it makes sense to have free, secure Wi-Fi in the office. The password can be posted or obtained from the receptionist.

Patients should not have "unexplained waits." Knowing how long a wait will be enables the patient to tolerate it better. This is why you hear "your expected wait time is X minutes" on telephone queues. It's always less frustrating to deal with the known than the potentially infinite.

Ideally, the check-in receptionist would know how the doctor is running and be able to tell the patient an approximate wait time.* Alas, this would require a degree of communication between the "front" and "back" staffs that will be unrealistic to expect until implanted chips enable them to read each other's minds. However, *we* can tell our assistant to inform the front desk how delayed we might be and to communicate that to the patients as they check in.

Even better is going into the waiting room ourselves. I frequently did this on my procedure days, when it's almost inevitable that I'd be running behind in my schedule. Between cases, I'd go to the waiting room, sit down next to a patient awaiting an endoscopic procedure and explain truthfully in a voice just loud enough for others in the waiting room to hear† what the delay was and about how long I expected they'd be waiting.

This technique accomplishes several things: it addresses Maister's "uncertain" and "unexplained" waits; it lets the patient know that *I* know he's there and that I care about his time; and it sends the same message to every other patient in the waiting room—the doctor cares.

---

* "The doctor will see you soon" doesn't cut it.
† Being mindful of HIPAA regulations, of course.

Oh, and I always, *always* overestimated the wait time to the patient. That way, if I got delayed, I was still within the time period I mentioned, so no goodwill was lost. And if my patient was brought to the procedure room earlier than I'd predicted, he received better service than expected.

Finally, research shows that how a waiting period ends affects how the wait is perceived and remembered.[7] So if the patient is taken back sooner than expected by a medical assistant who greets her personally and warmly, the patient will have a less negative recollection of the wait.

Beware that staff can end a wait badly. Remember my "you're going to sweat a little" experience that opened this book.

A DOCTOR PREPARES*

MY TEENAGE DAUGHTER ZOË NEEDED an ACL repair after injuring her knee while dismounting from the balance beam in her gymnastics class. We were waiting, a bit anxiously, in the day-op's preoperative area for the orthopedist. The surgeon, who had a top-notch reputation, breezed into our curtained-off little area, looked no one in the eye, and opened with, "Okay, which knee is it?" I wanted to shout, "You don't f——g know?"

With our help, he identified the knee, initialed it, and walked out with barely a word to the anxious patient and family he left behind. Now, you and I could pick that interaction apart, but I want to concentrate on one aspect: He didn't seem to know who Zoë was or why she was there.

Remember from Chapter 4, What Patients Want, that patients want us to know them, but you and I both understand that it's simply impossible to remember everyone we see and what their medical problems are. So what do we do? We look through the chart or scan the EHR. But for Pete's sake, not in front of the patient! First, it clearly demonstrates that we don't know them medically, and second, the patient knows that

---

* With apologies to Stanislavski.

we are not fully listening to him if we're simultaneously reviewing the medical record. We are not fully present.

Corinne Case, a wonderful physician's assistant from northern California, told me a charming story about remembering people. There was a gas station owner in her town who hired a young man to fill the customers' cars with gas.* The owner was surprised to see that after working there for only a week, the new attendant was greeting all the customers by name. They loved him. A prodigious memory? No, technique. When he saw a customer for the first time, he would write the customer's name on a piece of masking tape and surreptitiously stick it to the car's gas cap. The next time the customer came in for gas, he was greeted by name.

For us, the first thing we should do in setting the stage is to know whom we are seeing: review the patient's chart *before we go into the room.* This should take maybe thirty seconds, even if we just look at the problem list. Even better, quickly review the note from the last visit. Perhaps an additional twelve seconds there.

Now, here's a technique that I suspect you may already use, but which we should do with every patient. Sometimes, in the course of a visit, a patient will incidentally mention a bit of personal information: a planned vacation, a child heading off to college, or perhaps an ill relative she's worried about.

As soon as you can after the visit, note that event in the chart. In the antediluvian days of paper, I'd put a Post-it note in the chart with the information the patient had told me. When EHR came in, there was a little area at the top of the screen called "FYI," where information could be entered that was not part of the official record.

With these personal tidbits in mind, you can start the next visit weeks or months later with a question like, "Before we get started today, how was your trip to Vegas?" Or "How's Johnny doing at University of ?" Or "How's your mother feeling?" This personalizes the visit and

---

* Yes, youngsters, that was a regular practice once.

demonstrates to the patient that we know him as an individual and not just another body coming through the door.

Patients really appreciate such gestures. Many have complimented me on my "amazing memory." Even though I may not have one, personalizing the visit in this way is still an example of authentic behavior in a manufactured environment—good performance.

MAKING YOUR ENTRANCE

THERE ARE TWO COMPONENTS TO making a good entrance: stopping and going. It's so easy during a busy, pressured day to go into autopilot mode. We move from room to room, patient to patient, with barely a pause between. Many years ago, I said to my then-wife, "Some days I just act like a running back: I put my head down, pump my legs as hard as I can, and power my way to the goal line." That's not exactly conducive to personalized customer service. Nor to a successful marriage, I might add.

Perhaps the most important thing we can do to ensure a good performance for our next patient is to stop and collect ourselves and get back into character. In his fine book, *Time to Care: How to Love Your Patients and Your Job,* Dr. Robin Youngson says, "…the first step in finding time to care is simply to stop. Give your patient complete attention. Bring stillness to your mind and be attentive to what is happening. Magic happens in these precious moments."[8] I could not have said it better myself, which is why I let him say it.

Stopping takes but a moment as you stand outside the room. A deep breath or two will help still your mind and redirect it. Take a few seconds to imagine yourself being and then becoming the biggest, best version of your physician self for the patient you're about to see. And then…

Smile.

I've never understood why so many practitioners enter the patient's room with a businesslike, "professional" demeanor. Are they trying to be impressive? Are they showing the patient they understand the magnitude of the situation? Are they seizing control of the appointment? Maybe they're just worn out and trying to get to the goal line.

A serious deportment accomplishes nothing and may even be detrimental. A Cleveland Clinic study showed that patients actually want caregivers to be happy as they treat patients. As Dr. James Merlino, formerly Chief Experience Officer of the Cleveland Clinic, puts it, "A caregiver's negative expression may... make patients wonder whether there is something of concern with the conditions or care: 'Is there something Dr. Merlino is not telling me?'"[9]

Now, think how every great entertainer makes an entrance—with a smile, with confidence, with body language that says, "I'm glad to be here."* Howard Thurston, one of the great touring magicians of the early twentieth century, used to stand behind the curtain before every performance and repeat aloud over and over, "I love my audience. I love my audience. I *love* my audience." And they loved him back. I'm not recommending that, but even for those patients whom we don't particularly care for or who always have difficult visits, it's possible to greet them warmly and with a smile.

A genuine smile. A Duchenne smile. Who? Yes, he of muscular dystrophy fame, even though he wasn't really the first to describe the disorder.† It turns out that Duchenne also studied the physiology of facial expressions.

A genuine smile involves both the raising of the corners of the mouth by the zygomaticus major muscle and the raising of the cheeks with crinkling of the corners of the eyes by the obicularis oculi. An authentic smile results from the voluntary contraction of the mouth muscles *and* the involuntary contraction of the obicularis oculi. A zygomaticus-only smile looks fake, the "Say Cheese" smile, as one author put it.[10] If we try to voluntarily contract the obicularis along with the zygomaticus, the

---

* Watch this video: https://www.youtube.com/watch?v=I-TYsaN1vmY. Even George is smiling.

† A somewhat irrelevant, but historically necessary fact. The first description was by Giovanni Semola some twenty-seven years before Duchenne. But I digress.

result is a pained expression, far from a Duchenne smile. You simply can't fake a genuine smile. But you can feel your way into one.

Another characteristic of a genuine smile is that it builds slowly. British body language expert Mark Bowden teaches that it takes about three seconds for a smile to develop. He points out, "A smile is a universal signal for 'It's all good,' and is a very safe way to signal to the majority of people on our planet that they can feel safe with you." [11]

To make an entrance that will put your mind in a good place and put the patient at ease, first pause to collect yourself and clear your mind, act as if you are about to see a good friend whom you haven't seen for a long time, let that good feeling suffuse you, and that warm Duchenne smile will naturally appear.

This is how performance technique creates authentic behavior and, thus, good performance.

TAKEAWAYS

96 PERCENT OF PATIENT COMPLAINTS are about the customer service, not the doctors.

THE VENUE
- Is it easy for patients to get to and park?
- What impression does the decor give?
- Is the office warm and welcoming?
- Is it kept neat and clean? Any brooms in the corner?

SUPPORTING CAST
- Remember that staff are dealing with patients at their worst.
- Their "customer service" job is much harder than ours.
- The doctors set the tone of the office.
- Kindness and respect toward staff will result in kindness and respect toward patients.
- How would you want your mother to be treated?

AUDIENCE MANAGEMENT

- The doctor or medical assistant should keep the front staff informed as to how far behind the doctor is running.
- Patients should be informed truthfully about this.
- Productively occupy patients' time and "get them started" with a simple questionnaire in which they list their three principal concerns for today's visit.
- Offer free Wi-Fi.
- Make sure there are no unexplained waits.
- Go into the waiting room yourself to explain a delay to a patient; all the others will take note.
- Overestimate the wait time.
- Be sure of a good ending to the wait.

A DOCTOR PREPARES

- Review the chart, at least the problem list and the last visit, before you go in with the patient.
- Review "personal tidbits" the patient has told you and bring them up at the very outset of the visit.

MAKING YOUR ENTRANCE

- Take a moment to take a breath and collect yourself outside the exam room door. You are preparing to be in the moment and get in character.
- Smile. Act as if you are about to see a good friend you haven't seen for years, and that warm Duchenne smile will naturally come out.

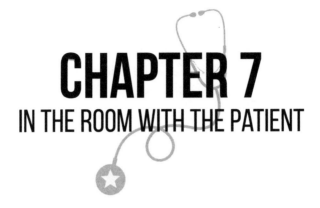

CHAPTER 7
IN THE ROOM WITH THE PATIENT

THIS IS THE ROOM WHERE it happens, where the magic of medicine takes place: when two people are together in a room, face-to-face, talking, listening, relating, communicating. This is where the healing begins. But we are the ones who have to make it happen. The time when the doctor and patient are alone together is what this book is really about. Everything else is preparation for this moment.

One important aspect of doctor-patient communication is body language, and in this chapter I want to concentrate on the unconscious messages we send to patients with *our* body language. I consulted with Charles "Buck" Adams, certified body language expert and Instant Influence trainer. Buck kindly offered a few body language techniques particularly relevant to physicians. The basics are in this chapter, and you can find details straight from him in Appendix II.

As you read the suggestions, you may be thinking to yourself, "I already do this." If so, great! You may pat yourself on the back contentedly as you read. If you used to do these things but have fallen out of the habit, this chapter will be a helpful reminder. If you've never done what I'm suggesting, well, there's no time like the present to start. You have nothing to lose but so-so ratings.

But first, a cautionary tale. The very first thing to do before you walk into the room is check the door. Make sure the door latch and lock are functioning. One of my partners didn't and paid the price. There was a patient in our practice whom we all liked, but whom I'll admit we all dreaded seeing. I'll call her Rose because her personality was big and brassy, like Mama Rose's in the musical *Gypsy*, and because that was her name. She wore a "rose" perfume that lingered in everyone's noses long after she had left the office. Rose was kindhearted and affable, but she had the extraordinary ability to extend even the most routine visit into a marathon. She accomplished this simply by talking nonstop at near the speed of light about whatever came to mind. Attempts by physicians to intervene by asking questions or redirecting her were fruitless. Often it was necessary literally to back out of the room smiling and close the door to end a visit.

One day my partner Michael Cohen tried to execute this maneuver, but the door handle malfunctioned, and it was impossible for him to open the door and escape. Nor could the door be opened from the outside. He gamely listened to Rose while having an allergic reaction to her perfume for an hour before the locksmith arrived. Rose told everyone it was the best doctor visit she'd had in our office. Alas, this was in the days before ratings.

We offered the normally unflappable Michael the rest of the day off.

THE GREETING

ASSUMING YOU'RE NOT SEEING ROSE, I hope you've entered the room with a warm smile, feeling genuinely glad to see the patient. It is, after all, a privilege to have the patient's trust.

What you say in greeting will depend on the relationship you have, or don't have, with the patient. If you're new to each other, you'll have to decide how to introduce yourself. Your choices are two: either as Dr. So-and-so or with your first and last names. For myself, if the patient were significantly older or younger than I, I'd say, "Hi, I'm Dr. Baker." (The "hi" was intentionally informal.) If the patient appeared to be about the same age as me, I'd say, "Hi, I'm Bob Baker." (The "Bob" was intentionally informal.) These are always said looking the patient in the eye.*

These choices were age-appropriate. Older patients are used to calling physicians by "Dr.," and younger patients have learned to greet their elders by honorifics.† Contemporaries use first names. This pattern worked for me over the years, but might not work for you. Whatever your choice, your goal should be to establish an immediate connection with the patient.

At a point in the relationship that feels comfortable to you, you'll need to establish more formally how you and the patient are going to address each other. I'd start that conversation by saying to my contemporaries or older patients, "I like to be called 'Bob' or 'Dr. Bob,' whichever you prefer. I think Dr. Baker is way too formal. How do you like to be called?" I'd always address the issue first to introduce informality right away. Of course, not all patients, and particularly not older ones, want informality, so it's necessary to be flexible.

I recognize that my approach may not be right for you or your patient population. You're welcome to search the literature on the subject[1] and decide what you think would work best. However you decide to proceed, the goal should be to create a warm, friendly, and comfortable relationship with the patient.

The handshake goes a long way toward establishing that relationship. We've all experienced how unpleasant a poorly executed handshake can be. One of my patients always offers a very limp hand. It feels so passive and perfunctory that it prevents any connection from being established. This man, although very talented and well-trained on paper, has difficulty getting any jobs that entail an interview. On the other hand (sorry), I have a certain group of patients—elderly Mediterranean-born men—who seem to feel it's a point of honor to try to crush my hand with their steel vise grip. Or maybe their intention is to render me incapable of performing a colonoscopy on them. I don't know.

---

* More on exactly how to do that later.
† Millennials excluded.

There are three types of handshake: dominant, submissive, and neutral. In the first, you forcefully turn your hand palm down as you shake the other person's hand, exposing the underside of his wrist. This is a very aggressive handshake and has no place in the realm of healthcare. In the neutral handshake, both shakers' hands remain vertical and the grip strengths match. Buck Adams points out that this is the "*safest* way to go."

I often used a firm, but welcoming, handshake in which I rotated my hand to the right, turning the underside of my wrist up and letting the patient's hand assume the more dominant position. At the same time, I'd gently pull his hand toward my abdomen, unconsciously demonstrating that I was comfortable exposing my vulnerable abdomen to him. I found that this handshake, accompanied by a warm smile, almost invariably led to friendly, productive visits.[*]

SIT OR STAND? AND WHERE?

HOW WE POSITION OURSELVES RELATIVE to the patient is important for two reasons. First, it establishes the relative status of doctor and patient. Second, it affects the passage of time.

Say what?

As you'll recall from Chapter 4, patients want us to give them enough time and the more the better. Alas, time is always short for us. If we had more to give to patients, we would. I think wistfully about the colleague I mentioned in the Introduction who allots thirty minutes to every single patient. Sigh.

However, here's something darned near magical: If you sit while talking with the patient, he will perceive that you are spending more time with him than if you stand. Researchers at the University of Kansas Medical Center conducted a study[2] wherein doctors visiting patients post-operatively either sat or stood at the bedside. Patients

---

[*] See Buck Adams's additional comments in Appendix II.

overestimated the amount of time both sitting and standing doctors spent with them, but on average credited sitting doctors with spending 50 percent more time than those who stood. This was despite the fact that the sitters actually clocked about a third less time with the patients than the standing docs.

As a magician, I love this. You are creating the illusion of spending more time with patients without lengthening your day or rending the space-time continuum. Evidence-based magic!

The next question is how to position yourself relative to the patient. Sometimes the situation will dictate this, as when we visit at the bedside.* In the consulting office, most doctors sit in their chairs opposite the patient with their large, impressive desks between them. This arrangement, known as the competitive/defensive position, is fine for being deposed[†] or negotiating a peace treaty[‡]. In the office, it creates a barrier between doctor and patient.

Much better is for each person to sit at the same corner of the desk so that doctor and patient are both facing inward and toward each other:

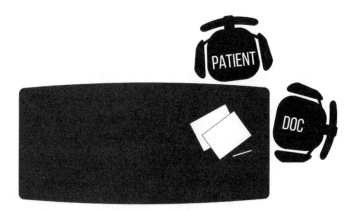

---

* Way back when, I actually sat on the foot of the patient's bed. Then I decided I didn't want to be a fomite.
† Been there, done that.
‡ But not that.

This positioning allows for good eye contact as well as observation of gestures. Also, it brings the two people closer together while keeping a partial barrier between them and preventing the invasion of each other's space.

In the exam room, space tends to be at a premium, so an important concern is the relative levels of the doctor and patient. Most authorities recommend that they be at eye level to each other, giving them equal status and enabling them to make good eye contact.

My approach was different. As long as the patient was physically stable, I would have her sit on the exam table, and I would sit on a small stool with my head height lower than hers. This put the patient in a dominant position and gave her the feeling of being in control.

This positioning was a physical expression of my career-long philosophy that the doctor is a hired expert advisor, and that the patient is the boss. I never believed in "doctor's orders," but rather "doctor's advice." I learned this from one of my mentors, the late Carroll Behrhorst, MD. I did a three-month, medical-school elective at his tiny clinic in Chimaltenango in the mountains of Guatemala, where I helped care for the poverty-stricken Cakchiquel Indians, direct descendants of the Maya.[*]

"Doc" Behrhorst, speaking at Oxford University in England in 1976, said, "The mystique and power of the doctor must be placed within their proper context, and the role of the physician defined as a true collaborator and true healer by functioning as a teacher—to teach the patient to be capable of responding to himself. I would like to emphasize that the doctor of medicine is *not* the custodian of health as is commonly supposed, but the *patient* is the keeper of his own health, life, and death." Doc was a man ahead of his time.

Think carefully about what you want your relationship to your patients to be and position yourself accordingly in the exam room. You might consider you and the patient to be co-equal partners in their

---

[*] https://www.youtube.com/watch?v=N3zYv7Taqq8

healthcare, in which case you will want to be on the same eye level. If you are comfortable with the patient feeling in charge, put yourself a little lower. Most likely, as you "read" your individual patients, you'll want to adopt one strategy with some patients and the second with others. I hope that we can agree, though, that towering over the patient is probably not conducive to a good therapeutic relationship.

Your foot position, whether you are standing or sitting, can also convey information unconsciously to the patient. Again, check Buck's advice in Appendix II.

GETTING DOWN TO BUSINESS WITHOUT GETTING DOWN TO BUSINESS

OKAY. YOU'VE GREETED THE PATIENT and sat down. Now what? I've been to doctors over the years who've asked, "What's up?" or "What seems to be the problem today?" or "What brings you in?" These all strike me as curt and seem to imply, "I don't have much time, so let's get to it."

Rather than asking the patient a question, it's better to start with knowledge. For instance, there are the "personal tidbits" I mentioned in Chapter 6, Setting the Stage. One might say, "Before we get started today, how was your trip to Vegas?" or whatever the tidbit is. If you know why the patient has scheduled an appointment, you can refer to that and then add: "I know you're scheduled for a blood pressure check, but are there other concerns you want to bring to my attention?" Here you could refer to the "Three Questions" sheet the patient might have filled out while in the waiting room.

Even for a patient you're seeing for the first time, it's possible to start with knowledge. "I looked over the history you filled out and reviewed your medications.* How may I help you today?"

That last sentence is crucial and one I arrived at over time after asking it many different ways. Key to the sentence is the "may I." You

---

* You *did* look it over before entering the room, I hope.

are in essence asking permission to be of service to the patient, which is, I believe, our role as physicians. Further, you are demonstrating humility, so essential in the helping professions.

Your tone of voice is as important in connecting with patients as what you actually say to them. In a study in which surgeons' discussions with patients were analyzed for tone of voice (content was filtered out), independent judges were able to correctly determine which of the surgeons had been sued for malpractice, as opposed to those with no history of lawsuits. The judges were able to make the distinction simply by listening to ten-second clips of the surgeons' tone of voice.[3] Those surgeons whose tone was "dominant" were much more likely to have been sued than those whose tone was warm.

But how do we achieve a "warm" tone of voice? It comes from acting as if. In that moment before stepping into the room, pausing and acting as if you are about to see a good friend whom you haven't seen for a long time will give you the warm feeling that will translate into a warm tone of voice. Feel it, and thereby become it.

You'll recall from Chapter 4, What Patients Want, that the number one characteristic that patients desire in their physicians is that they be good listeners. So let's look at some easily applied techniques that let patients know that we really are listening.

EYE CONTACT

MAKING EYE CONTACT IS ONE of the most potent ways humans can bond, but it has to be done the right way. We'll get to that in a moment. There is excellent evidence that prolonged eye contact itself releases oxytocin, the so-called "cuddle" or "love" hormone in the human brain—at least when you do it with your dog.[4]

Many writers claim that human eye-to-eye contact and conversation also release oxytocin, but I've been unable to find any specific substantiating studies. However, when men with high-functioning autism (formerly called Asperger's syndrome) are administered intranasal oxytocin, they make more eye contact with other people than they usually do.[5]

Whether human eye contact releases oxytocin or not, making eye contact is undoubtedly important in establishing a relationship with another person. What do you feel when someone repeatedly avoids eye contact or averts his gaze? Not comfort or connection, that's for sure.

It's important for us to make eye contact with our patients, but we must do it effectively.* Locking eyes continuously with someone quickly becomes creepy, to use the technical term.

Instead, body language experts recommend that we use the "social gaze," which signals active, friendly listening. Imagine an inverted triangle with the baseline connecting a person's eyes and the apex being just below the mouth. This is the area of the face to look at, scanning from the eyes to the mouth while listening. Actual eye contact should occur about 60 to 70 percent of the gazing time.

We want to avoid "power" gazing, in which the triangle is flipped to put the apex on the upper forehead. This type of eye contact, where we scan from the eyes up to the forehead, makes people distinctly uncomfortable.†

CONVEYING EMPATHY: THE TRIPLE NOD AND REFLECTING

I KNOW YOU'RE EMPATHIC. *YOU* know you're empathic. But how do you let the *patient* know?

First, here's a great way to demonstrate that you are truly listening to the patient. It's called "the triple nod." Three slow and deliberate nods of the head convey active, engaged listening. The proper rate of

---

* In some cultures, direct eye contact is considered rude, so be sure to take the patient's background into account.
† To remind myself of this, I have only to think how my father would look at me if I brought home a "B+" on a test.

nodding is hard to describe; you have to feel it. But be aware that if the nod is too slow, it suggests you're bored. If it's too fast, you are signaling impatience or excess agreeability. Feel genuinely interested, and the proper-speed triple nod will happen naturally.

To convey empathy, tilt your head to the side *as* you do the triple nod. Most of us listen more intently with one ear or the other, so tilt your head toward the side of your more active listening ear as you nod.

"Reflecting" means repeating the patient's words back to him, either exactly or paraphrasing. To do this, you need to listen for the basic meaning and emotion of what the patient is saying and then repeat that back to him. You don't need to reflect everything he says, of course, but it is very useful to do so when you feel the patient is saying something that is emotionally important to him. For instance, if a patient says to me, "I'm worried about the colonoscopy," my instinct might be to say, "Don't worry, I've done thousands of them." That's a useless reassurance because it's dismissive and disrespectful. Also, it's ineffective to respond to an emotion with a fact.

Better would be if I said, "You're concerned about the procedure. Yeah, I was worried before my first colonoscopy, too. What particularly concerns you, the procedure itself or what I might find?" This response demonstrates that I have heard the patient's concern, understand and respect it, and want to help resolve it.

What you may well notice with the triple nod and reflecting is that, not only are you conveying empathy to the patient, but you are feeling it more yourself. Both these techniques do that. To paraphrase the earlier quotation from Jerry Sternin: It's easier to act your way into a new way of feeling than to feel your way into a new way of acting.

LET THE PATIENT SPEAK

WE HAVE ALL EXPERIENCED THE frustration of listening to the patient whose history is a long, wandering narrative pretty much devoid of useful information. A patient like Rose, for instance. However, even with a patient who is not long-winded, physicians convey impatience by interrupting between twelve[6] and eighteen[7] seconds after she starts speaking. Such interruptions convey failure to listen and, worse, lack of respect for the patient. My advice on this topic is simple: Restrain yourself.

SET POSITIVE EXPECTATIONS

My friend David Crone was the director of network and telecom for Ohio Health, a major healthcare system. Before that, he was the senior technical director of network operations for data for AOL. He has since moved, as he says, "from the C-suite to center stage" and is now a wonderful full-time ventriloquist. We met several years ago at the annual Vent Haven "ConVENTion," a yearly gathering of ventriloquists from all over the world.[*]

David is writing a book on lessons from show business for corporate leaders, and we were comparing ideas in our books. David made a great point that could also apply to physicians about setting expectations and being positive. He told me, "I'll often say to an audience, 'We're going to have a good time tonight. This is going to be fun.' And later I'll reinforce it by telling the audience, 'Man, you guys are great! This is such a fantastic audience.' Sometimes, they're not, but you can convert people to being a good audience when you teach them to be a good audience.

"Being a patient, I think a doctor should walk into the office and tell you the things you're doing right. Sometimes I dreaded going to the doctor because I thought, 'He's going be angry with me and tell me again I've got to lose weight and I'm doing this wrong and I'm doing that wrong.' So we got a new family physician who is much better

---

[*] One of the many reasons I love going is that it's great to be with five hundred people who don't think you're weird for being a ventriloquist.

about this. He points out what you're doing right and says, 'Hey, that's working. Keep doing that.'"

Interesting that David cited weight loss as an example, because over the years I've helped many patients lose weight. I would be struck when a patient's opening statement was, "You're gonna yell at me because I gained weight." And I would say, "In all the time we've known each other, have I ever yelled at you?" They would admit I hadn't, and we would discuss what had happened and why. I'd frame the situation positively, talking about how hard it is to lose weight, and what a great job they'd done so far, and how I was confident they could pick right up again and not "let a lapse become a collapse." That is so much more effective than frowning or displaying disappointment.

There really is nothing to be gained by scolding patients, no matter how angry we may feel when they've ignored or even flouted our advice. It is always possible to put things positively, to build the patient up and encourage him and to say, "I'm really looking forward to seeing how well you're doing next time you come in." As David Crone says, tell the audience they'll be great, and they will.

WHAT TO DO ABOUT THE DAMNED COMPUTER

THIS FAR INTO THE BOOK, can you guess how I feel about electronic health records? If not, extrapolate from how you'd imagine I'd feel about having to listen to "It's a Small World After All" for forty-eight hours.

Yes, I know all about the advantages of instant access to all the patient's data, about the legibility of the notes, and about the ability of multiple physicians to share the same "chart."

But I also remember how in medical school I was taught the art, yes, the *art*, of taking a history and performing a physical and then writing them up succinctly and skillfully so that other physicians would have a good understanding of the patient and her problems. Try to do that in whatever EHR program you've been sentenced to use.

Remember, the primary goal of EHR programs is not to help you, but to help the billers. Your needs just get in the way.

But we're stuck with the damned things, so let's figure out how to make the best of a lousy situation to benefit our patients and ourselves.

First, it's important to remember that while we are listening to and observing our patients (Acting Technique #1), they are observing *us*.[8] They are responding to *our* eye contact, tone of voice, and body language. What message are we unconsciously (or consciously!) sending when we're hunched over our iPads or pecking away at the keyboard? Simple: that getting the information into the computer is more important than listening to the patient.

The computer even gets in the way of both sides' verbal communication, as an Israeli group demonstrated. They found that "gazing at the monitor was inversely related to physician engagement in psychosocial questioning and emotional responsiveness" and that "keyboarding activity was inversely related to both physician and patient contribution to the medical dialogue."[9] But then you know that from your own experience with the computer.

Yet we're required to get the data into the computer. So here are some suggestions as to how to find a balance between listening to the patient and making the necessary computer entries.

Way back in 1984, Professor Christian Heath of the University of Surrey in England suggested explaining to the patient beforehand that we will have to intermittently enter information in the computer and that we then wait for opportune moments to do so. While the patient is speaking, we direct full attention to her. When we type, the patient remains silent.[10]

Drs. Wendy Leebov and Carla Rotering address how to handle the computer in their excellent book *The Language of Caring Guide for Physicians*. (I'll discuss their work further in Chapter 12, What Others Say.) They suggest alternating your mindfulness between the computer and the patient; attend fully to one and then the other. As Dr. Theo

Tsaosides reminded us in Chapter 2, multitasking is impossible: You can direct your full attention to either the computer or the patient, but not both.

Leebov and Rotering caution that if the patient brings up a critical piece of information or something emotional, you should turn completely away from the computer to direct your full attention to her. They further suggest letting the patient see the computer screen so she knows there are no secrets. This also makes it evident to the patient when you have logged out, ensuring her privacy.

I had tried variations on all those strategies to keep the computer from getting between my patients and me. As I mentioned, I had learned to touch-type so well and so quickly that I never had to look at the computer screen or the keyboard. However, none of these solutions felt satisfactory. The technology was always there, always coming between my patients and me.

The solution I finally came up with was extremely low tech and very effective: a clipboard with paper on it and a pen. When taking the history, I would jot quick, one- or two-word reminders on the paper that would enable me to reconstruct the history right after the visit was over. They were just memory joggers. For instance, no history of nausea, vomiting, diarrhea, constipation, hematochezia, or abdominal pain was "ō NVDCHP."

I could jot quick notes, immediately look back up at the patient, and keep my concentration on her. Showing patients my pen, I'd tell them that I had decided to use "a primitive analog device" to record their histories, and they seemed relieved by this "old-fashioned" way of doing things. They'd generally give a knowing, relieved chuckle. Right after the appointment, I'd dictate a cogent narrative note right into the EHR, completing the medical record quickly.

I found this technique took no more time than trying to enter notes into the computer in the exam room, gave me a more coherent note, and was greatly appreciated by patients. Win, win, win.

THE PHYSICAL EXAMINATION

PERFORMING THE PHYSICAL EXAM CAN break the channels of communication between doctor and patient that taking the history had established. Although in one sense the physical exam is very personal, an entering into personal space that is the physician's special privilege, the disconnection occurs because the doctor stops talking. This is natural because there are places on the body to scrutinize and palpate and sounds to be listened to. The physical exam needs our full concentration to be done well.

However, this leaves the patient passive and wondering what's going on, what the doctor might be finding. Also, on routine examinations it's easy for us to lose our own mindfulness, to "zone out" while performing an examination we've done thousands of times.

I used two techniques to overcome this. Sometimes I'd tell the patient, "During the examination, I'm going to be concentrating hard on what I'm doing, so I won't be talking for a few minutes. I'll explain everything when I'm done." And I'd double down on my own mindfulness. During more casual, "well-baby" exams, or with anxious patients, I'd narrate the physical, explaining what I was doing and finding as I went along. Of course, if I found something concerning, I would not mention it at that moment.

YOUR EXIT

YOU'VE DISCUSSED YOUR DIAGNOSIS AND plan, ordered labs, sent in prescriptions, answered patient and family questions, summarized the information[*], and you think you're finished. As you start to leave, you wait for the dreaded "doorknob question," the one asked when your hand is on the doorknob, about to open the door. You're relieved when it doesn't come, or perhaps a little annoyed when it does.

---

[*] Even so, patients only remember about 30 percent of what they're told in a doctor's visit.

Let's back up a little. First, there are several ways to ensure that patients understand what has occurred in the visit. These include summarizing the instructions, writing them down, having the patient take notes, reviewing the patient's "three problem" sheet, and having the patient repeat a summary back to you. I've used all of them at different times, depending on the patient and the complexity of the problem.

However, there were two questions I always asked before leaving. Their wording was the result of trial and error until I found the exact phrasing to achieve the result I wanted—finishing the visit in a way satisfactory to both the patient and me.

- "Does our plan sound reasonable to you?" Getting the patient to express her "buy-in" to the planned diagnostic/therapeutic course is important to increase the likelihood of compliance with that plan.
- "Are there any other questions you want to ask me or any other concerns you want to bring to my attention before I go?" This clearly signals the end of the visit to the patient and gives him one last chance to voice a concern. Far and away, the most common answer was "no," but even when it wasn't, questions were usually minor and quickly answered.

If the patient brought up something of importance, of course I had to make a snap judgment as to whether or not it could wait until another visit. Sometimes an issue would be raised or an emotion expressed that necessarily stopped my schedule in its tracks. There's nothing we can do about that except address the problem. Or be a lousy doctor.

I always ended the visit with some type of touch, depending on my relationship with the patient: a warm handshake, a hug, or a gentle squeeze of the patient's elbow. And I always acted as if (and therefore felt as if) I were leaving a good friend and let my smile show that.

THE ROLE OF HUMOR

As a professional ventriloquist and comedian, I'd be remiss (to myself, at least) if I didn't touch on the role of humor with patients. Few things can ease the atmosphere of any human encounter like humor. *But* there are four rules to know:

1. If people have not found you funny all your life, the exam room is not the place to start trying to be. There are open mic nights for that. Good luck.
2. All jokes should be at your own expense. All. Every. Single. One.
3. Rated G. Not PG-13, G.
4. If you violate any of these rules, I will send angry ventriloquist puppets to your house late at night. Believe me, you don't want that.

Thank you.

Okay. You've left the room and closed the door behind you. But the performance is not over.

TAKEAWAYS

The Greeting
- Enter the room genuinely glad to see the patient; it is a privilege to do this work.
- Choose the familiarness- and age-appropriate greeting.
- Use a neutral or "welcoming" handshake that conveys warmth and trust.
- Tell the patient how you like to be addressed; ask his preference.

Sit or Stand? And Where?
- Sit during the visit to give the perception of spending more time.

- In the consulting office, sit at the same corner of the desk as the patient.
- Be careful of the positioning of your feet.
- In the exam room, sit at or below the patient's eye level.

GETTING DOWN TO BUSINESS

- Remember who's the boss. Be humble.
- Start the conversation with knowledge: personal tidbits or medical.
- Keep your tone of voice warm, not dominant.

EYE CONTACT AND CONVEYING EMPATHY

- Use the "social gaze," making eye contact 60 to 70 percent of the time.
- Do the triple nod to show active listening.
- Tilt your head to your active listening side during the triple nod to convey empathy.
- Reflect back to the patient important or emotional content.

INTERRUPTIONS AND EXPECTATIONS

- Let the patient speak; don't interrupt in twelve to eighteen seconds.
- Accentuate the positive.

THE DAMNED COMPUTER

- Don't let the computer get between you and the patient:
- Alternate your attention between the two or
- Use a primitive analog device.

THE PHYSICAL EXAM

- Narrate the physical.

EXITING

- Ask, "Does our plan sound reasonable to you?"
- Ask, "Are there any other questions you want to ask or concerns you want to bring to my attention before I go?"
- End the visit with a gentle touch.

THE ROLE OF HUMOR

- Use humor, if you know how.
- Or else I *will* send those puppets.

FINALLY

- Remember, the performance is not over.

CHAPTER 8
THE PERFORMANCE MUST GO ON

THE PATIENT EXPERIENCE IS NOT over when the exam room door closes behind us or we leave the patient's hospital room. First, there may be medical questions that could not be resolved during the visit. These require follow-up. Then there is the emotional residue we leave behind. Its nature will depend not only on what the patient's medical issues are, but also on how we've handled them. The goal of the previous two chapters has been to give you techniques and strategies that ensure patients feel satisfied and in good hands, even if all the answers are not in.

We may have physically left the patient, but there is still more we can do to enhance her experience. And I don't just mean ease of checkout and simonizing her car. One time after a patient visit, I even played God. Sort of. More about that later.

FOLLOW UP

IN RESEARCHING THIS BOOK, I interviewed some top-rated (by their patients) physicians to learn what they did that made their patients love them. Dr. JoAnne Gottridge, now Senior Vice President of the medicine service line at Northwell Health, told me, "The most important thing I do for my patients is keep my promises. When I tell them I'm going to do something, I do it." That seems rather obvious, doesn't it? But

I bet most of us have told a patient we'd call back with lab results and then gotten busy and forgotten.* Or maybe we've told a patient we'd call and then just dashed off a note or told an assistant to do it because we were pressed for time.†

Many health systems and medical practices allow patients to go online to find their own results, at least in states that permit this. Our practice had a "patient portal" where results became available to patients three days after they were reported, whether the doctor had "signed off" on the results or not.

"Oh, great," think many physicians. "Here come the panicked calls about a potassium of 5.1."‡ That actually turns out not to be most doctors' experience, but going online is simply no substitute for a call from a physician, nurse, or medical assistant.[1]

At one time I told my patients, "I'll have your results in a day or so. If you don't hear from me, everything is fine. I'll call if there's a problem." Totally unsatisfactory, I now believe. It leaves the patient without closure on the results and therefore wondering, "Am I okay, or did he forget to check?"

For years, before electronic health records, I used preprinted short notes on my letterhead that said,

Dear _____,

It was a pleasure seeing you during your recent visit. I'm pleased to inform you that all your results came back in satisfactory range.

Sincerely,
Robert W. Baker, MD.

---

* Yep. Been there, done that.
† That, too.
‡ Note to orthopedists: that's very slightly elevated, but generally not of concern. No extra charge for the snark.

I'd simply fill in the name and add a signature that reflected our relationship (Dr. Baker or R. Baker or Bob). I'd usually add a quick personal note at the bottom, like "Glad the news is good!" or "Let me know how you're doing," or something appropriate to a holiday season. The wording of the letter intentionally covered those lab results that weren't strictly within the normal range, but which I knew were inconsequential. Of course, there were the occasional "What does 'satisfactory' mean?" phone calls.

Now, with EHR, we can easily send patients notes and lab results right from our computer to theirs. There is, however, some resistance from patients of a certain age: "I don't know how to use the computer. My grandson helps me."

Dr. Gottridge also keeps a tickler file to remind her of promises she has made to patients. Most EHRs offer reminders that pop up on our desktop on a certain date. Okay, there are one or two things I like about EHR.

In truth, the technology doesn't matter. The promises do. We need to keep them.

UNDER-PROMISE. OVER-DELIVER.

THIS IS ONE OF THE great mantras of business, and it certainly applies to ours. In short, we can set up patients' expectations so that we at least meet them and sometimes exceed them. For instance, if I removed a polyp during a colonoscopy, I'd tell that patient I'd have the results in a week. This allowed for lab delays, weekends, and so on. Often, the results would come back faster than expected, so if I notified the patient sooner than a week, I delivered better than expected service. If, in fact, the results took a full week to come back, nothing was lost.

Remember, we also discussed this technique as it applied to informing patients of waiting times. Inform the patient the wait will be a bit longer than we actually think it will be. There's a good chance we'll get the patient in sooner than promised and thereby over-deliver.

Both of these examples are rather easy and simple ways of managing patient expectations, but this becomes more crucial when discussing important medical issues. The literature is rife with studies demonstrating that the more a physician meets a patient's expectations in a visit, the better the clinical outcome and the more satisfied the patient.[2,3] However, in addition to trying to figure out the patients' expectations, as the studies advise, we can also *proactively* set and manage patients' expectations of their doctor's visit and, more important, about the outcome of their illnesses. There are plenty of articles full of advice on managing patient's expectations, and, while their counsel generally strikes me as accurate and on point, no research backs up their suggestions.

That said, here's my advice.

It's important to remember that many patients will have unrealistic expectations about their medical outcomes, whether they are seeing you for a URI, to figure out troubling symptoms, to solve a medical mystery, or to treat them for a serious condition. They've watched medical shows on TV where brilliant doctors make great diagnoses and all turns out fine in forty-six minutes plus commercials. They've read all about their illness on the Internet and believe they know what needs to be done. Or they've been told by a referring friend that *you* are the only doctor to see. Good luck with that.

Second, we need to be humble and know our own limitations. After all, our understanding of the human body and its diseases, as comprehensive as that knowledge may be, is far from complete.* Our treatments are even less so. Hence, we need to be honest with patients about what we can accomplish for them. And by doing so, we can avoid disappointing them.

---

* I have never forgotten this admonition from the first day of medical school: "We know that half of what we are teaching you is wrong. We just don't know which half."

Third, we need to remind patients that we cannot predict the future, that everyone is different, and that nature has a way of surprising us.

Those are my ground rules. Now let's use them to apply *under-promise, over-deliver* to three clinical situations.

1. The patient has what you've determined to be a viral pharyngitis but is requesting an antibiotic. Having said the following hundreds of times, I know it by heart: "I wish I had something that could cure this for you, but your symptoms and the tests indicate that this is viral, and antibiotics don't help. That said, although I can't make this go away any faster, there are lots of things we can do to help you *feel* better while you are waiting to *get* better." (Here I would give the patient printed information on the symptomatic treatment of all the URI symptoms he's likely to get. The sheet also listed warning symptoms for which the patient was to call immediately.)

   "What will probably happen is that over the next several days the sore throat will improve, but you'll get a stuffy or runny nose and then a cough. With the cough, you're going to bring up some mucus, but it will probably be clear or light yellow, so don't worry about that. Don't be surprised if the cough lingers for a few weeks, even after you feel just about all better. This is common. Be patient with your body and you *will* get better. If anything seems to be going the wrong direction, call me."

The picture I've outlined for the patient is the worst-case scenario for an uncomplicated viral URI. I've anticipated and proactively addressed the expectation for an antibiotic and changed it by describing the likely clinical course and giving the patient a concrete plan for symptom relief. He leaves knowing what to expect and what he can do about it. If all the symptoms I've described come to pass, then I'm a pretty good predictor. If they don't, he's done better than he expected. I under-promise, his body over-delivers.

2. The patient asks, "How long will this take to get better?" I answer, "I can't tell you exactly. Everyone's body is different, and everyone responds differently to treatments. Some people get better in (fill in typical time course); others take more or less time. But remember that the course of recovery from anything is never a straight line upward." I trace a straight line ascending at a forty-five-degree angle on the office wall or in the air as I talk.

"It's a zigzag line, with plateaus of no improvement, and even setbacks along the way, but the overall trend is upward. (I trace a jagged line.) You may not notice that you feel better each day, but as time goes by, ask yourself, 'Do I feel better today than I did a few days ago, or a week ago?' I think you'll find that you will."

Once again, I'm describing a typical, if slow, recovery for virtually any illness or surgery. The patient's knowing what to expect prevents that "hey-I'm-not-better-yet" phone call.

3. The patient wants to know, "How long does Dad have?" I say gently, "I wish I could tell you, but over the thirty-five years I've been doing this, I've learned that nature has a way of making a liar out of me. Sometimes I think a patient is going to do well, and then something totally unpredictable happens, and that's it. Other times, the situation looks dire and the patient keeps chugging along, doing okay. There's just no way to know.

"But what I can tell you with certainty is that we'll have the best people doing everything medical science can for him. We'll give him every chance in the world to get better and then we'll have to see what happens. But know that I will be with him and you every step of the way."

Regarding the last sentence, please refer to the preceding section on keeping promises.

In setting expectations, it is crucial not to *over*-promise, *under*-deliver. My urologist (he of the Teutonic nurse from the Introduction) over-promised and under-delivered. He told me, "A vasectomy is really a very simple procedure. I have guys playing basketball the next day."

Well, the next day I was lying in bed in a Percocet haze with ice packed between my legs. I remember thinking, "I want to meet those guys. Those are some *real men*."

MOMENTS OF PATIENT ASTONISHMENT

These are actions, minor or major, that surprise patients because they simply would not expect a doctor or other health professional to do such a thing. They come out of the blue and have a positive effect far exceeding the energy required to perform them. As Dr. Robin Youngson puts it, "Tiny acts of loving-kindness are the bedrock of a happy and fulfilling practice."[4]

Here are some actions requiring minimal effort, but which patients remember:

- A patient mentions that his wife is pregnant and is due in six months. Put a reminder in the EHR to call them in seven months to inquire about mom and baby.
- Same for a patient's child celebrating a major event such as a graduation, confirmation, or bar/bat mitzvah.
- Send a handwritten congratulatory note.
- Send a handwritten condolence note to a patient, even if you don't know the relative who died.

Don't use services that send a "handwritten" note for you. They may seem like a great time-saver, but can come back to bite you on the bum. When my father passed away, I received what I thought was a lovely personal note from an acquaintance. I was quite touched. Two weeks later he sent me an email advertisement for an automated note-writing service he was associated with. I was quite pissed.

These moments of patient astonishment require a bit more effort:

- In her book, *The Perceptive Patient*, healthcare consultant Brooke Billingsley tells of arriving back in her hospital room after a mastectomy to find a bouquet of flowers from her surgeon.[5] He did this for every patient.
- Pay a condolence call. This is hard for us when we lose a patient. I had wondered how families would regard my showing up at a wake or a shiva. Would they on some level blame me for the patient's death? Would I blame myself, even if I'd done everything right and everything possible? Without fail, though, over the course of thirty-five years, families were deeply grateful for my coming and for the efforts I'd expended on behalf of their loved one. Their sentiments helped soothe my grief.
- If a patient has a life milestone and is active in a charity, make even a small donation in his honor. If you prefer, make a donation to your favorite charity in his honor. Do some good; get a deduction.

Then there are the stories of providers who go way out of their way to accommodate a patient and thereby create a memory never forgotten:

- When my wife, Marcia, was delivering her son, a nurse who had worked a double shift was attending her in labor. When the nurse's shift was over, she stayed an extra hour to help Marcia through the delivery. Thirty-eight years later, the nurse has undoubtedly forgotten my wife. Marcia has never forgotten her.
- My friend, Philadelphia attorney Joey Masiuk, remembers the night in 1983 when his wife's young obstetrician came in on

his day off to perform an emergency C-section because he'd promised Joey's wife that if she needed a section, he'd do it. In keeping his promise, the doctor missed taking his board certification examination that day.

- A patient of mine who knew about this book wrote me: "In June of 2016, my fifty-year-old son tragically and unexpectedly took his own life. The shock and stress on me took its toll and several visits to my doctor were required. When I divulged to Dr. X what had brought these sudden medical problems on, his response overwhelmed me. He showed deep compassion and understanding to my wife and myself, hugging and consoling us, something I will always be grateful for." This episode put Dr. X an hour behind in his schedule.

I am sure you have your own such stories. When you retire, your patients will recount to you your kindnesses to them, and you won't remember having done them.

COMPLAINTS, REVIEWS, AND SURVEYS

AS WE DISCUSSED IN CHAPTER 1, patient satisfaction surveys and online reviews are now a part of our professional lives. They are not going away and will probably become even more prevalent. They will affect how much we get paid and whether we can retain our patients and attract new ones. Some insurance companies are considering removing poorly rated doctors from their panels.

I want to address two major questions surrounding reviews. First, how do we respond to poor reviews? (And as fine physicians as we may be, we are going to get them.*) Second, how, besides implementing the techniques and strategies in this book, do we get good reviews?

---

* Been there, gotten those.

Face it: bad reviews hurt. Even if they're about our practice and not specifically about us, they are personal. Being physicians is not just what we do, it's who we are. So criticism cuts to the core of our being. Also, we know much more about medicine than the patients do, so it's galling if they question our medical judgment or treatments.

When hurt, our first response might be to strike back or to answer defensively online. Don't. Responses posted in anger are responses we'll later be angry at ourselves for having posted. So the first thing to do is take some time to cool down.

Next—and this is, I know, a lot to ask—consider if there is some truth in what the patient posted. For instance, until my patient Mr. Anderson from Chapter 5 posted about my escorting him to the X-ray machine without offering him a gown, it had simply not occurred to me that male patients might have a problem with that.

Allowing that a certain patient might be correct in his criticism may be hard, since most online reviews and surveys are submitted anonymously. Even if you can't identify the patient, however, consider whether he is bringing up a problem in your office or a behavior or attitude on your part that warrants reexamining.

If you do know who the patient is, it's best to deal with the problem offline. The last thing you want to do is engage in a public flame war with a patient. In the eyes of the world, you'll lose.

Some online critics actually enjoy duking it out on the Internet. For instance, in the literary world there are self-appointed "librarians" on the social media site Goodreads who have compiled a list of "Badly Behaving Authors" and stalk them online. You don't need that.

Sometimes a phone call to the patient with an explanation and an apology can go a long way toward smoothing out a fraught situation. An apology does not imply personal culpability; rather, it expresses regret for a less-than-ideal experience.

A positive response online will work in your favor. An apology and explanation along with a listing of what steps you'll take to prevent the situation from arising again shows the patient and, crucially, every other person who reads the bad review that you respond well to criticism and learn from it. It shows you care.[*]

One real problem can be false or fraudulent reviews. Sometimes doctors have sued patients over these, and they've generally lost.[6] Review websites usually will not remove negative reviews at a doctor's request, so I'd say consult your lawyer as to how to proceed.

For a good discussion of how to handle negative reviews, I recommend *Hug Your Haters* by Jay Baer.[7]

One thing that can counter a negative review is lot of positive ones. I think it's completely reasonable to ask patients to post positive experiences online. You may feel uncomfortable personally making this request. No problem. At check-out the secretary can hand the patient a little card that says, "If we served you well today, would you consider posting a rating or review online? Some sites are: HealthGrades.com or RateMDs.com, or Angie's List or Yelp! If you feel we did not meet your expectations today, please speak to Nancy, our administrator, so we can correct the situation. Her direct phone number is..."

The health system I worked for sent Press Ganey surveys to random patients after their visits. I would explain to patients that they might receive a survey in the mail or online and that it would be very helpful to me if they filled it out. People receive surveys all the time and most folks ignore them. However, if you make it clear to the patient that filling out the survey is important to you, it will be important to them. (Keeping track of these reviews will also help you gauge the effectiveness of what you've learned from this book in improving your patient ratings.)

Several years ago, I took my car to the Chevrolet dealer for service. Posted prominently in the waiting room was a blowup poster of the survey that Chevrolet would be sending customers after the repairs were completed. The dealership had filled in every answer space with

---

[*] I remember from a mandatory malpractice prevention course I took years ago that we were instructed not to say, "I'm sorry I did___," but rather, "I wish that hadn't happened." Be careful not to use words that may come back to haunt you when some lawyer reads them to you on the stand in court.

a large, red A-rating and instructed customers to fill out the survey that way. Because of that, I didn't. They've since gone out of business.

We should never tell patients how to fill out the survey. However, as you may know, in Press Ganey and other surveys, only a "top box" rating counts in your favor. The score they report is the percentage of patients who check the very highest rating. So if you score a *nine out of ten*, it might as well be zero. I think patients need to know this because they might think that giving you a nine is being helpful to you when it's not. Therefore, after explaining how the survey works, I believe it is ethical to say, "I hope you will give me the highest rating you think I deserve."

PLAYING GOD—SORT OF.

IN THE CASE I'M ABOUT to describe, the performance was truly not over even after the patient had left the office. I had a patient I'll call Sandy of whom I was very fond. He was a burly guy, a former vaudevillian, and an inveterate smoker. He had heart and lung problems, poor circulation, and any other number of problems associated with smoking. For years, I'd tried every way I knew to get him to stop. Finally, after an exacerbation of COPD that landed him in the hospital, he came for his follow-up visit and promised, really promised with all sincerity, that this time he'd finally given up cigarettes. He seemed quite proud of himself, and I congratulated him.

It was a lovely spring day, and I had the window of my office wide open to enjoy the warm breeze. My office window was right above the exit door of the building, and I happened to look out to see Sandy's wife pulling up in their car to pick him up. There was Sandy, about to get into the car while lighting a cigarette.

In a moment of inspiration, I summoned up my deepest, most stentorian voice and called out the window, "Sanford Goldberg, this is God speaking! Do I see you breaking your promise to the doctor already?" Sandy looked up and all around but couldn't see me. Looking a bit dazed, he crushed out the cigarette and got in the car.*

Sandy died several months later. His wife told me that after that day he had never smoked again.

TAKEAWAYS

- Keep your promises.
- Under-promise. Over-deliver.
- Manage expectations proactively.
- Provide moments of patient astonishment.
- Consider asking patients to write online reviews.
- Learn from negative ones. Let the patients see you've learned.
- Explain to patients how surveys work.
- Ask them to give you "the highest rating you think I deserve."
- Play God when necessary.
- At your own risk.

---

*When my wife read this story in my manuscript, she asked me if I had *really* done that. "I absolutely did," I said. She said, "You would."

CHAPTER 9
MORE TECHNIQUES TO TRY:
IMPROVISATION AND STORYTELLING

A PATIENT ONCE ASKED ME why I was ordering just a few diagnostics for him and not a "whole battery" of tests.

"Why don't you just order everything? What do you think is going on?"

I realized that the patient was not asking for a differential diagnosis, but rather inquiring as to how I was going to solve the mystery of his illness. I improvised a story on the spot:

"Imagine you tried to turn on your television set and it didn't work. You would make a list in your mind of possible causes: Is the TV plugged in? Does the remote control need new batteries? Did a circuit breaker trip? And then you'd check out each of those things. You'd look behind the TV to check the plug. You'd change the batteries in the remote. You'd run down to the basement to check the circuit breakers. And you'd examine each possible cause until you found and corrected the one problem keeping you from watching TV.

"Well, I'm doing the exact same thing with you. I have a list in my mind of maybe ten things that could be causing your symptoms, and I'm ordering tests to eliminate them one by one. There's no point ordering an expensive test to determine if, say, number eight is the problem, when simpler tests might determine that it's number two or three, just as you wouldn't immediately bring the set in for service until you'd checked the simpler possibilities."

He got it.

This chapter on additional techniques is elective. You will improve your patient ratings and your personal satisfaction practicing medicine if you treat every patient encounter as a performance and adhere only to the practices suggested in Chapters 6 through 8. If you do that, however, you'll miss the opportunity to have some fun learning about improvisation and to participate in a group project in which the readers of this book will be able to help each other by sharing the therapeutic stories they tell to patients.

"IMPROV" FOR PHYSICIANS AND OTHERS

WHEN YOU THINK OF THEATRICAL improvisation, you probably think of comedy. You may have heard of or seen performances by the great improv groups like Upright Citizens Brigade, The Groundlings, and Second City. These shows provide nonstop laughs, but, somewhat paradoxically, the performers are not trying to be funny. The humor comes from the situations onstage, which grow out of the often absurd scenes the performers are creating on the spot.

In my own improv training at Upright Citizens Brigade, starting right from Improv 101 class, we were taught not to think ahead or go for the funny line or the silly action, but rather to remain true to the scene we were creating as it unfolded.

What characterizes improvisational theater is that it is created spontaneously and cooperatively. Though there is a structure to certain forms of improv, there is no script, and none of the players know exactly what is going to happen until it happens—kind of like a doctor's visit.

Improv theater never repeats itself. The scenes the performers create have never happened before and will never happen again. Every performance is unique unto itself—kind of like a doctor's visit.

A crucial element of improv is that it is cooperative. The performers work together; that they support each other and not compete with each other is the most crucial component of success. Improv is created in the moment, and the only way it works is if the improvisers listen carefully to each other, respect each other's choices, and respond in the moment—kind of like a doctor's visit.

And, for that matter, kind of like life.

The use of improvisational theater training to enhance medical professionals' communication and empathy is becoming increasingly prevalent.[1] Even businesses like Google, PepsiCo, and MetLife are training executives in improv, and business schools are including it in their curricula.[2]

Professor Katie Watson of the Northwestern University Feinberg School of Medicine is a lawyer who teaches bioethics at the school, and she is also an experienced improv performer and instructor at nearby Chicago's Second City. She teaches an elective course on what she has called "medical improv" for medical students to help them sharpen their communication skills with patients. Commenting on the connection between "improvising and doctoring," she says, "Physicians and improvisers are driven by the same paradox: the need to prepare for unpredictability. Improvisational theater teaches its practitioners to accept uncertainty and ambiguity as the conditions in which you must perform, rather than reflexively trying to impose order on something that has not yet unfolded."[3]

Really, we are improvising just about every moment in our lives. We are taking in everything going on around us and responding in our own characters, or whatever "self" we are being at that moment. One big difference between life and improv theater is that, whereas in life we may choose to express disagreement with what another person is saying or doing, in improv we always say "Yes, and…"

Yes, and is at the core of improv. As Upright Citizens Brigade teaches, "'Yes' refers to the idea that you should be agreeing with any information your scene partner gives you about your reality. 'And' refers to the adding of new information that relates to the previous information."[4]

In real life, we are often tempted to say, "Yes, but." That doesn't exist in improv. Cooperation is crucial to the mindset of the improv performer in order to advance a scene. For instance, this conversation would never happen in improv:

> *Player A: The playground is empty; let's shoot some hoops.*
> *Player B: I'd rather play stickball.*

Player B is not accepting the premise that A has established that they are going to play basketball. In improv, we might see:

> *Player A: The playground is empty; let's shoot some hoops.*
> *Player B: (starts bouncing an imaginary ball) I'm glad I brought my basketball.*

Here, Player B has accepted that the scene is going to be based on playing basketball and adds the information that he has a ball. Player A might then say, "Here, pass it!" and hold his hands out to catch the ball. And so forth.

In the exam room, we may not agree with everything a patient says; but by applying the principle of *Yes, and,* we can create a cooperative encounter that advances the agendas of both doctor and patient. By way of example:

> *Patient: I'm really tired of taking all these medications.*
> *Doctor: Yes, but with your blood pressure you absolutely need to take them.*

The doctor's *Yes, but* response dismisses the patient's concern, cuts off any further communication about medications and sets a negative tone for the rest of the visit. The principle of *Yes, and* would produce a completely different scenario:

Patient: *I'm really tired of taking all these medications.*
Doctor: *I get that. I hate having to take my own meds. Let's talk about what we can do to help you take fewer pills.*

In improv, all parties are responsible for helping each other toward the goal of a successful scene or outcome. That's what *Yes, and* embodies. For us, the *Yes, and* response creates a visit where doctor and patient are going to work together to achieve a common goal. Which approach— *Yes, and* or *Yes, but*—would you think is more likely to satisfy the patient?

The improv philosophy of *Yes, and* is being adopted in many fields, including business, as I noted earlier. Tony Schwartz, writer and business consultant who helps companies solve intractable problems, wrote in the *New York Times* about the eye-opening experience of his own improv training:

"...starting with 'yes' energizes, creates safety and trust and fuels creativity. I learned this viscerally during an improvisation workshop, run by the Magnet Theater, at a recent company offsite meeting. One of the basic tenets of improvisational comedy, it turns out, is to start with 'yes'—and even more specifically with 'yes and.' When you work with someone in a scene, your challenge is to resist disputing, challenging, or negating whatever your fellow actor says, and instead embrace, work with and build on it.

What I realized quickly was how good it felt to say 'Yes and,' and how much more smoothly it made the scene move forward."[5]

For physicians, the strength of improv training is that it improves communication and enhances empathy.[6] To learn more, I spoke with an expert in the area. Mike Ganino is a corporate culture and experience expert who has trained and performed with Second City, Upright Citizens Brigade, and Improv Olympics. Mike also has extensive experience with the medical world, having had type I diabetes for twenty-nine of his thirty-eight years and dealt with all the attendant doctors' visits and hospitalizations.

Mike regularly trains medical professionals in improvisational theater, with universally positive responses from doctors. Many physicians, including those who are reluctant to perform, find the improv exercises simple to do and easy to apply to their daily practices. They find themselves "really listening" to patients in a way they had not before. Mike told me, "What we're really diving into, the things we want to help with are empathy, listening, communication, and influence."

One of the improv exercises Mike employs is known as "Rip Van Winkle." In it, two participants have a discussion in which one is a modern-day person and the other is someone who fell asleep, say during the Civil War, and has just awakened in the twenty-first century. The first person is given a modern-day object, such as a cell phone, to explain to "Rip" in language he'll understand, considering that he's missed one hundred fifty years of progress. "Rip" gives feedback if the explainer uses language or terms he's not familiar with.

Mike explains, "Doctors live so much in all the information and knowledge that they have that communicating to a patient can become a little 'jargony' and the patient has no idea what they are talking about. After doing the Rip Van Winkle, one of the doctors I was training had an Aha! moment when he recalled that just the day before he was talking to a patient about a shunt, and he realized that the patient had no idea what he was talking about."

Other improv exercises include labeling emotions and mirroring another person's words and actions. All are geared to "reading" the other person, opening back and forth communication, and helping each other. Mike reports that many of the physicians who have taken his training feel there was a great "return on investment" of their time. As one put it, "The workshop was frightening, exciting and super helpful. Going back to my practice afterwards, I was really looking forward to connecting with patients and remembering why I got into this [field] in the first place."

I wish I could quickly teach you improv so that you could incorporate its skills into your practice, but it can't be taught on paper. It would be like trying learn how to perform a physical examination without a live person to examine. You could read printed instructions again and again, but you'd never learn how to *really* do it without a human to practice on and a teacher to correct your errors. Similarly, improv is a physical and mental exercise that has to be performed live with other people if you want to learn to do it skillfully.

So I urge you to contact a local theatrical improvisation group and take a class with them. Just say *Yes, and.*

STORYTELLING AND THE DOCTORS' STORY BANK

TAKING A PATIENT'S HISTORY IS essentially gathering enough information to create the story of his illness. It's our job to take the usually incomplete and disjointed information the patient offers and compile it into a logical narrative. As we do so, we discover gaps and unanswered questions which, when filled in and answered, can lead us to a correct diagnosis. As physicians, we have to understand patients' stories.

We can also use our own stories and analogies as powerful tools to help and instruct our patients. It's an effective technique because humans are hardwired for stories. Storytelling exists in every culture and probably goes back to the dawn of humans. Professor Uri Hasson of Princeton has shown that the functional MRIs of people *listening* to a story align nearly exactly with the fMRI of the person *telling* the story.[7] In popular lingo, when we tell stories to each other, our brains are in sync.

Every professional speaker knows the powerful effect stories have on an audience. The famed Disney Institute, where business leaders from all over the world go to learn Disney's corporate culture and customer service methods, says, "…as we at Disney Institute have taught countless organizations and professionals over the years…when used effectively, storytelling can positively impact any step-by-step process within an organization."[8]

Over the thirty-five years I was in practice, I developed stories and analogies like the one that opened this chapter to illustrate points to my patients. Some of them I used to persuade people to take a particular action or to convince them of my point of view. Others served to amuse them and break the ice. I could easily adapt the stories to each patient's individual situation. You probably have stories like that, too; I imagine every doctor does. So let's share them.

With this book, I am starting the *Doctors' Story Bank*. You can find it at www.ThePerformanceOfMedicine.com. Click on the *Doctors' Story Bank* link. There you will find not only my stories, but also those of other physicians and providers that you can use with your own patients. You may use any of the stories you find there with your patients, but I ask that you not publish others' stories elsewhere. It's our resource for the readers of this book. See how to submit your own stories at the end of this chapter. I'll start by including my best stories here:

DIFFERING ADVICE FROM DIFFERENT PHYSICIANS

We've all had patients seek second opinions and receive diagnostic and/or therapeutic recommendations from other practitioners that differ from ours. Or we refer a patient to a specialist who offers one plan, and then the patient sees another specialist who suggests something seemingly totally different. Patients want to know how this can happen. Here's the story I tell them:

Suppose you had a piece of land and you decided to build a house on it. You go to two different architects and say, "I want a house with four bedrooms, two-and-a-half bathrooms, a family room, a dining room, and a front porch where I can watch the world go by." Each architect would come up with a different design. Each would meet your needs, but they'd be different.

The same is often true in medicine. There's seldom just one way to solve a problem, and each doctor will come up with a plan based on her knowledge and experience and what has worked in the past. That doesn't mean one is right and the other wrong. They both can solve the problem, just differently.

SETBACKS IN RECOVERY

Patients recovering from surgery or an illness sometimes perceive they're having setbacks or days when they don't seem to be improving. Once I've determined that no untoward medical event has occurred, I explain progress this way:

> The course of recovery from anything is never a straight line upward. [Here I'll trace on the wall with my forefinger a straight line moving upward at a forty-five-degree angle.] It's more of a zigzag line with improvement, plateaus, and dips, like this. [I trace a zigzag line upward.] This is normal and can feel discouraging. Instead of seeing if you are getting better day by day, ask yourself, "Am I feeling better than I was a week ago, or two weeks ago or a month ago?" I'm certain the answer will be yes.

For patients who have children or grandchildren, slow improvement can be explained like this:

> You don't see your kids growing every day, but if your parents haven't seen their grandchildren for several months, they always remark how much they've grown. So on a day-by-day basis, you may not see much improvement, but I haven't seen you in a couple of months, and you are doing much better than last time.

SUDDEN DETERIORATION IN CONDITION

One of the most distressing things for a family is when a patient, usually elderly, suddenly gets worse and seems to be heading for a cliff.

When I was a medical student at Columbia, we admitted a ninety-seven-year-old history professor with a broken hip. At his age, he was active and spry and had all his marbles. He was still writing and teaching. He walked to work every day from his apartment up Riverside Drive to Columbia, and one winter day he fell on the ice and broke his hip. When we admitted him, he was absolutely fine, except for his hip. He had uneventful surgery to fix it, but then a minor complication set in, and then another, and another, each worse than the last. Ten days later he was dead.

For the elderly, a seemingly minor incident can be like an avalanche. It starts with a pebble coming loose. That one hits others and they start to slide down the hill, and they hit more, and soon the whole mountainside is coming down. That's what can happen with old people. They seem fine from the outside, but they're old on the inside, and a minor event can trigger an avalanche.

THE RECALCITRANT PATIENT

You might—just might—have patients who don't take your advice and return with same problem again and again. For such patients, like inveterate smokers with recurrent upper respiratory infections or refluxers who just *have* to have that bowl of ice cream as a bedtime snack, this story has worked for me. Be aware, though, that it must be related goodnaturedly and with a smile on your face, because you are making just a bit of fun of the patient:

I walk over to a wall of the exam room and start to rhythmically knock the side of my head against the wall. I say:
You know, Doctor, I have terrible headaches all the time.

I stop knocking my head and continue, now playing the role of me:

Well, Mr. Jones, if you stop banging your head on the wall, they might go away.

I resume knocking:

Oh, no, Doctor, I can't do that. I like banging my head on the wall.

That might fall a little outside your comfort zone, but for the right patients, it does knock a little sense into their heads.*

WHEN PATIENTS INSIST YOU PRESCRIBE AN UNNECESSARY MEDICATION OR TEST

This is a potentially fraught situation, because the patient has made up his mind that he needs something, like an expensive test or an antibiotic for a viral URI, and won't be satisfied until he gets it. You explain your medical thinking, and he doesn't accept what you say. The patient can perceive your refusal as intransigence, as your not caring or wanting to be bothered, or any number of things that are untrue. This approach can work:

Let's just stop for a moment. You know, the easiest thing in the world for me to do would be to simply write the prescription, and you'd get what you want and walk out happy. Quick and done, no sweat off my back. Instead, I've just spent all this time explaining to you why I don't think it would be in your best interest medically. I've risked pissing you off, making you resent me, and maybe even causing you to leaving my practice, when all that could be avoided in thirty seconds just by giving you a prescription. But I didn't do that because my sole interest here is what, based on my knowledge and thirty-five years of experience, I think would be medically best for you.

---

* If you do use this story with your patients, I take no responsibility for any self-inflicted concussions or subdural hematomas.

ACHES AND PAINS

As my patient population aged, I heard more and more complaints about life's daily aches and pains, and how annoying they were. I would commiserate:

I know. I get them, too. I was complaining to my wife, Marcia, about them, and she said to me, "We both have friends who died way too young. And wouldn't they gladly exchange some aches and pains and wrinkles and sagging skin for more time with their families and friends?" When I think about it that way, I accept what's going on and feel happy about it.

GRATITUDE

We all go through difficult times; I certainly have. When patients express discouragement about the track of their lives, I tell them about my friend John.

John was a wonderful surgeon who operated on two of my kids. He was a gentleman and a gentle man, and he developed leukemia at age fifty-two. I visited him in the ICU, and we talked about good times we had shared. I returned to my office and two hours later I received a call that he had died.

The next morning, just after dawn, I was walking to my car to go to work. It was a beautiful, crisp fall morning with a cloudless sky and perfect sunrise. I looked at the sky and inhaled the fresh morning air and thought to myself, "John will never experience another sunrise like this, and I can. I am so damned lucky."

TURNING SIXTY

It's one of life's big milestones, though for those of us who grew up listening to the Beatles, perhaps an even bigger one is sixty-four. When patients brought it up and lamented the passage of time, I'd relate this story:

I remember when I turned forty I said to myself, in baseball terms, "You know, pal, you could be rounding second base." When I turned sixty, I said to my ex-wife, "Does this mean that I'm rounding third and heading for home?" She smiled, patted my arm and said, "No, you had a collision with the shortstop."

I AM EAGER TO SHARE your stories and analogies with our fellow practitioners. You can submit yours for addition to the *Doctors' Story Bank* by emailing them to Stories@ThePerformanceOfMedicine.com. You, of course, retain the right to publish them elsewhere.

TAKEAWAYS

- Improv is a valuable skill in medicine and in life.
- "Yes, and" is more effective than "Yes, but."
- Stories and analogies are powerful tools to help connect with patients
- Contribute your stories and analogies to the Story Bank.

SECTION III

MOVING AHEAD

CHAPTER 10
PUTTING IT ALL TO WORK

IF I HAD STOPPED TO consider what percentage of the advice I've read in self-help and "how to" books I've actually put into practice, I might never have started writing this book. I guess it's every author's wishful thinking that his or her readers will be enthralled with the material in a book and put it all to use. A bit of self-reflection now quickly disabuses me of that notion.

But it's too late to turn back, so let me try to help you implement at least some of what you've read about to improve the experience for both you and your patients on a day-by-day basis. And I do mean "at least some," because I fully recognize that not every tip, technique, strategy, and suggestion will appeal to everyone. And some of the things I've written about, you may already do. Or used to do. Or don't want to do. All okay with me.

That said, I believe the more you do, the better your performance will be and the better the experience for the patient will be. I have used every technique and strategy in this book, which is why I can recommend them to you.

Before getting into specifics, though, let's talk about good habits. Contrary to the popular belief that it takes about three weeks to form a new habit, it actually takes from eighteen to two hundred and fifty-four days (average, sixty-six) for a new behavior to become automatic—that is, a habit.[1] So anything in this book you decide to use will probably take about two months to become routine behavior for you. And I suspect that, if you try to do too much at once, none of it will become routine.

As I said earlier, I believe you're already a fine physician. So I'd say that the first thing to do is to note which techniques and strategies you already use and congratulate yourself for those. Then, I suspect, there are others that you used to do and, in the stress of a busy practice, have simply gotten out of the habit of doing. Revive them. Finally, look through the "Takeaways" at the end of Chapters 6, 7, and 8—the "before," "during," and "after" the visit chapters. See if one, maybe two, suggestions from each chapter particularly appeal to you, resonate with you (if we want to get touchy-feely about it). Write them down on a Post-it note on your desk to remind you every day of the new habit(s) you're forming. Move the Post-it around every day or rewrite it so that you take note of it every day and it doesn't fade into the routine background of your life or the clutter on your desk.*

If you can't decide which suggestions to select, either because they're all so excellent or so loathsome, I'd suggest the following:

- Before entering the room: Check personal tidbits and smile.
- In the room: Sit down and make good eye contact.
- After the visit: Follow through and under-promise/over-deliver.

These will at least get you started, but as they become routine, I hope you'll add more of them every couple of weeks to months, constantly striving to give your patients a better experience. Try to pay active attention to how patients are responding to you and to how you feel about your visits with them. I'm confident you'll see improvement in both.

Some of the suggestions might feel downright uncomfortable for you. For instance, when my former Chief of Medicine, Dr. Tom McGinn, first talked about going into the waiting room to explain being

---

* I might be projecting here.

late to a patient, I thought that was about the last thing I wanted to do. I feared that it would take too much time and that other patients would want to talk to me or ask me questions. None of that happened. All I got back from patients was gratitude.

Similarly, it was very hard for me to make myself break away from the computer and go back to taking notes with a pen and pad. I was sure I would forget what a patient had told me or would lose time dictating into the computer after the visit. Within a short time of trying the new-old system, I was very efficient, and the patients were much happier.

Most of all, I hope that you'll come to believe, feel, and incorporate into your way of interacting with patients the understanding that the patient visit *is* a performance. If you accept that notion and constantly try to be the best version of your physician self, then all the various techniques I've offered will become second nature.

KEEPING IT FRESH

I LEARNED A GOOD LESSON in doctoring from Paul McCartney, Sir Paul, if we want to get formal about it. My wife and I went to one of his shows and, aside from reliving the soundtrack of our lives, we also were struck by how fresh and personal the concert felt. If you consider how many times McCartney has played those songs and that there were eighteen thousand people in the venue, *fresh* and *personal* is quite an accomplishment.

How many times do you think he's played and sung "Yesterday"? A gazillion? Two gazillion? And yet he performed it tenderly, with as much feeling and soul as if he had written it last week. He played every song with enthusiasm and obvious enjoyment.[*]

At one point, McCartney asked us to give him a moment to "take you all in." He stood toward the back of the stage and scanned the room and nodded and smiled at the responses from the rear, sides,

---

[*] For the cynics who are thinking, "For what he's being paid, he *should* enjoy it," just stop! He's earned it!

and floor of the huge arena. It seemed he was saying, "I'm glad to be here with *each* of *you*."

Sir Paul personalized the show with stories and jokes that he told as if he were speaking to just one or two people. About the tour, he had told *Rolling Stone*, "The truth is when I do the show, I feel like I'm kind of talking to someone like me in the audience, even though you're at the back of the hall, we try and bring the intimacy to you... it's me, one-on-one, with every member of the audience."[2]

He does achieve that. But here's the most amazing part: When I saw the show, he'd been touring it for a year and a half around the world. And it *still* sounded fresh. Sir Paul was fully engaged with us. How does he do that, show after show, and what can we learn from him?

After all, much of what *we* do is repetitive too—the same history, the same basic physical exam, the same lab work. How many times do you think you've checked a patient's blood pressure? Thousands, probably.* How many labs have you checked? Sutures tied? EKGs read? So how do we keep our performance fresh?

I thought I'd ask an expert, British actor and Olivier Award-winning director Andy Nyman. (Sir Paul was not available.) Andy is one of those great working actors who has been steadily employed for thirty years. He has extensive film and television credits and, very important for our purposes, has acted in long-running shows in London's West End. I asked him how he keeps his performance fresh every night when he's been acting in a play for several months.

"The key and the simple answer is always *listening*," Andy said. "It's about listening to the person who's opposite you and not knowing what they're going to say next even though you've heard it a thousand times, because if you are genuinely listening, you can genuinely respond."

Listening and responding. I hope that sounds familiar. Andy also offered ways that physicians can stay in character. "How do you stay in the moment? By remembering that every patient is a new audience.

---

* Ophthalmologists, dermatologists, and plastic surgeons are excused from answering.

Reminding yourself before the [patient] walks in that they're coming in for your performance and you're about to go onstage and that this [doctor's visit] is of massive importance to them. So you ask yourself, 'Am I in character? Do I feel in the moment? Am I ready to enter into that scene?'"

Just as the actor must remember that every night there is a new audience and that no two audiences are the same, we can remind ourselves that no two patients are the same, even if they have the same medical problems. Every patient encounter becomes fresh and new.

However, Andy added, "Being in the moment and forcing yourself to be in the moment is a really, really difficult thing to achieve. Onstage, you have to disengage from everything else going on in your mind and just listen to what the person is saying. So I have always tried to put little tricks into my performances that allow me to be in the moment and allow me to be as present as I can be.

"One of the things I've always loved to do as a performer is what I refer to as being 'on my toes.' It requires making a physical shift. If you walk or stand naturally, you have your weight back a bit, on your heels. It makes you feel very grounded, but it also allows you to relax. If you shift your physical weight forward and take some of the balance off your heels and onto your toes, it puts a real spring in your step. It sounds like a cliché, but there's real life in it, and it literally forces you to be physically present."

This practice could be a problem for us since we've already learned that we should be sitting when talking to patients. However, you can achieve the same shift in balance and attentiveness simply by leaning forward in your chair.

Andy surprised me by mentioning something else that helps him keep his performances fresh: gratitude. He brought it up when I mentioned how Paul McCartney had taken time to appreciate the audience.

"He's one of the wealthiest people in the world, one of the most successful people in the history of songwriting, and yet he's still grateful and excited. He can still think, 'Oh, my God, look at the amount of people who are here to hear my songs.'

"I struggle with actors who aren't grateful and excited. I'm thirty years into my career and every time I do a job, I can't believe it, I'm excited, and I love it. That's one of the things that keeps it very, very fresh as an actor, even in a long run. I'm doing what I dreamed of [as a kid] every time I walk through the stage door. And for doctors it means reminding yourself every time you walk into the hospital or office."

How privileged we physicians are to do this! This is what *we* dreamed of as kids. And in the midst of the repetitiveness and the challenges and the hassles, how fortunate we are that this is how we are spending our energies and lives, in the service of others! One audience at a time.

TAKEAWAYS

- Forming new habits takes time, an average of sixty-six days.
- Reinstitute techniques you've read about here, but are out of the habit of doing.
- Choose a few new techniques and strategies and work on using them every day.
- Add new ones every few weeks to months.
- Make a mental note of how patients are reacting to you. Do you notice a difference?
- Remember, it's a performance!
- Keep your patient-visit performance fresh by listening and responding.
- Every audience, and patient, is different.
- The work we do is a privilege.

CHAPTER 11
WHEN THINGS GO WRONG

IT WAS THE TYPE OF phone call we all dread.

"Dr. Baker, I'm sorry to interrupt you while you're with a patient," said my secretary, Maria. "The ICU needs to speak with you right now about Mr. Peterson."

I apologized to the patient I was seeing and explained that I had an urgent call from the hospital. I stepped outside the exam room with the phone in my hand. What could be the problem? Mr. Peterson, a wonderful gentleman in his mid-seventies whom I'd taken care of for years, had been admitted with severe CHF and respiratory failure. He'd responded well to treatment and was on a weaning protocol to get him off the respirator. When I'd seen him on rounds that morning, he'd been progressing well.

The ICU nursing supervisor came on the phone. "Dr. Baker, I'm sorry to tell you that Mr. Peterson suffered a cardiac arrest and died."

"What? He was doing so well this morning."

"He had been put back on the respirator," the nurse explained. "A short time later he suddenly arrested. The team worked on him for a long time but couldn't get him back."

"Does the family know?" I asked.

"They were here."

"Okay. Thank you. I'll call them."

"Um, Dr. Baker?"

"Yes?"

"There's something else you need to know." The nurse paused. "When the respiratory therapist reconnected the respirator, he must have switched the tubes. The inflow and outflow tubes. That's why the patient arrested."

I was stunned. I honestly don't remember what happened next, the exact sequence of events, but I do know that I asked my secretary to have Mr. Peterson's wife and adult children come to the office to speak with me.

Recounting this story now, twenty years later, even to the keyboard, my heart is pounding. How I got through the rest of the day's patients, I don't know. Actually, I do know. By acting as if.

I had only one general plan going into the meeting with the family: Be open and tell the truth, consequences be damned.

At four p.m., my secretary ushered the Petersons into my consulting office. We all hugged, and I offered my condolences.

"I don't know how to tell you this," I began, "so I'm just going to tell you. There was a terrible mistake in the ICU, and that's why John had a cardiac arrest."

I explained what had happened the best I could with the understanding I had at the time. I answered all their questions. I told them how sorry I was. I shared their agony.

Of course, there was a lawsuit. As is their wont, the plaintiffs' attorneys named everyone involved in the patient's care—the hospital, the ICU doctor, the respiratory therapist, the equipment manufacturer—with one exception: me. I later learned that the patient's family had specifically requested that I not be named in the suit.

Mistakes are going to happen. Whether they're mistakes we make, or our staff make, or someone we don't even know makes, they will happen. And we know where the buck stops. Although some mistakes can be minor, such as miscommunicating an appointment time, in our business even the smallest mistakes can have dire consequences: a phone message misplaced, a lab result not checked or followed up on, an EKG misread, a polyp missed, a prescription written illegibly and filled incorrectly, a viscus perforated, a malignant lesion called benign and vice versa. I've seen all of those errors happen and committed a few of them myself.

It's strange how we forget most of our medical triumphs. When I retired, a long-time patient said to me, "You know, Bob, I switched doctors to you thirty years ago after you saved my mother's life." I smiled and said I was grateful to have been able to help. In fact, I had no recollection of the episode at all.

But the mistakes? They live on in our guts. They intrude into our thoughts at random times. They keep us awake many years later in the dead of night when they replay on an endless loop in our minds. They slap us in the face when we become complacent with our skills. Mistakes humble us when we think we're so smart and remind us how little about the workings of the human body and mind we actually know.

With any luck, we learn from our blunders, but, as the baseball pitcher Vern Law said, "Experience is a hard teacher because she gives the test first, the lesson afterwards."[1]

Mistakes, great and small, are an inevitable part of medical practice and the patient experience. What matters is what we learn from them and how we handle them. You have enough life experience to know how to learn from your mistakes. You wouldn't have gotten this far in medicine if you hadn't. Therefore, let's concentrate on how we can try to improve the patient experience, even when an adverse event—minor or major—has occurred.

But first, this necessary disclaimer: In case you haven't noticed, I am not a lawyer. I don't play one on TV or in print. **If one of your patients has an adverse outcome for which there is even a whiff of a hint of a chance that there could be a malpractice action, consult your malpractice attorney before taking any of the actions I recommend.** Back to regular font.

The first thing we have to do is tell the patient and/or family exactly what happened. This is difficult and embarrassing, to say the least. We fear the patient will leave our practice and tell others what happened. They will do both. In the Introduction, I wrote about the woman who supposedly died in the elevator leaving our office when, in fact, she had died coming up in the elevator before her appointment. *The false story is the one that spread around town.*

This illustrates the "grapevine effect." Over 50 percent of patients who have a bad experience will not complain to the practice about it. However, 97 percent will tell at least ten other people about it. Also, they can go online and tell the world what happened.

Well, too bad. We must inform patients. The Joint Commission requires hospitals to inform patients and families of bad occurrences, and we should follow suit in our practices. It's standard of care.

A nearly ever-present concern when something goes really wrong is a malpractice action. Here's some good news on that account. Studies at the VA Medical Center in Lexington, KY[2] and the University of Michigan Health System[3] demonstrated that, when medical errors were proactively disclosed to patients *and* the patients were offered compensation, malpractice claims and amounts paid out dropped significantly. Whether these hospital and health system studies would also apply to a private medical practice is not known. However, such an approach is surely worth discussing with your malpractice insurance carrier.

Finally, we have to think about ourselves and the embarrassment and humiliation of making and admitting mistakes. Dr. Lucian Leape of the Harvard School of Public Health says,

When we fail, it's very difficult. It's challenging to your self-image. That's true for everybody, but for doctors I think it's probably worse because they are so invested in producing a perfect product. They feel they've failed their patient and they feel they've failed themselves. A major failure in which you make a mistake and a patient is harmed is a blow to your ego, to your self-image, to your belief in who you are in a more profound way than we've been sensitive and aware of.[4]

Patients understand that we are human. They know we make mistakes. If they believe that we are always trying our best to serve them, they can be forgiving. Dr. Leape further states that there are four things patients want when a medical error has occurred:

- They want to know what happened.
- They want us to tell them we're sorry it happened.
- They want us to tell them we're going to find out *why* it happened.
- They want us to follow up with answers.

In less crucial episodes, such as botched appointment times, patients also want to know specifically how we intend to prevent similar mistakes or oversights in the future.

The issue of an actual apology is tricky. Traditionally, doctors have been discouraged from apologizing for fear that an apology would be considered an admission of guilt in a malpractice case. Fortunately, many states have passed "apology laws," which exclude apologies from being evidence in a court proceeding. Different states' laws have subtle differences, though. Some states, for instance, exclude admissions of culpability along with apologies from being used as evidence. In others, only the apology is protected. Check your local listings.

It is possible, nevertheless, to express regret without apologizing. "I wish this hadn't happened," is what I was taught in a risk management course several years ago. Or you can say, "What happened was terrible. I'm sorry it happened." Laws are evolving and changing, so, again, check with your hospital or practice's attorneys or risk management team. Do it before the next thing happens—because it will.

DEALING WITH ANGER—OURS

THIRTY YEARS AGO, EARLY IN my practice, I arrived home one Sunday afternoon tired and hungry after finishing several hours of rounds in two hospitals. No sooner was I in the door than the ER paged me. An elderly patient of one of my partners was there with what appeared to be an upper GI bleed. Would I please come and admit him?

Goddammit!

Of course, the man's daughter had taken him to the hospital that had no house staff, so it was all going to be on me. The patient was a somewhat frail man in his seventies, who was a little tachycardic and orthostatic but not in distress. The nurses had already begun fluid resuscitation, but no one knew if he was actively bleeding.

This was long before the days of urgent upper GI endoscopy to stop a hemorrhage, and it was standard procedure to drop a nasogastric tube and lavage the stomach to try to determine if there was still active bleeding. I explained this to the patient's daughter, but she refused to allow the procedure.

I pointed out that her father was capable of deciding for himself, after which she threatened to sue me and the hospital if I even went to him to talk about putting in the tube. I felt a bad moon rising.

I explained my rationale for the lavage and that her father had a potentially life-threatening condition, but she remained adamant, leaning toward hostile. I was starting to feel hostile myself. I asked the administrator on call to come speak with her. He came back reporting that the patient's daughter had found me arrogant and condescending.

I went back to talk to her, to try to make nice, and she told me that she wanted me off her father's case and that she had already called in a more experienced gastroenterologist to take care of him. "That's certainly your right," I said. (No, I snarled, actually.) As I walked away, she called after me, "Don't even think about sending me a bill!"

There are very few times in my life when I've felt truly enraged, but that was one of them. And to top it off, the ER paged me again to inform me that one of my own patients was there with chest pain.

I was not in a good mental state to see the patient, and there was no way I could avoid it. So I went outside and walked briskly around the hospital parking lot several times and tried to think calming thoughts until I had recovered my composure.

While this story is extreme, the fact is that patients or families or both can frequently anger us. They can be chronically late for appointments, demanding, noncompliant, and a plethora of other adjectives. They can add a note of unpleasantness to a day or ruin it entirely.

If we let them.

For me now, a five-minute break, a cup of tea, and an "it's showtime" reminder get me back on track to see patients with my normal cheerfulness. You probably have your own tricks and techniques to pull yourself back from anger and prepare for the next patient. In dealing with difficult patients, it can also be helpful to understand *why* they make us angry.

Clinical psychologist Dr. Norman Kanter offers some information from the field of cognitive psychology about how we can "change our view of an [angering] patient to a more positive one." I interviewed him, and you can find his valuable insights in Appendix III.

In brief, Dr. Kanter noted that cognitive psychology is based on the notion that our thoughts drive our emotions. Overly strong emotional reactions to a situation or patient result from "errors" in thinking.* The most common of these are:

- Judgmental *should* thinking along the lines of, "The patient *should not* have…"
- Losing perspective on the true significance of an event.
- Personalizing the event either by taking something too personally or by creating a negative image of ourselves because of the event.

Now, examining my own reaction to my patient's daughter, I see that I made all three errors.

---

* Dr. Kanter credited his colleague Dr. Dennis Gallo with creating this synthesis of the work of two of the giants of cognitive psychology, Drs. Aaron Beck and Albert Ellis.

- I decided the patient's daughter *should* have let me do the procedure I wanted (even though she was, from her perspective, looking out for her father's best interest).
- I lost perspective and forgot that the worst that happened to me personally was that I had to work a little more that day.
- I took her decision to have another, more experienced physician look after her father as a personal rejection of me and my abilities.

No wonder I was so pissed off!

You might well find that the next time a patient raises your hackles, considering these errors in thinking could be very helpful in reorienting yourself to get ready for the next patient. Again, you'll find full details in Appendix III.

TAKEAWAYS

DISASTERS

To handle disasters, I'll leave you with the recommendations of the Consensus Statement of Harvard Hospitals, *When Things Go Wrong. Responding to Adverse Events.*[5] It was written by a committee of physicians, lawyers, pharmacists, and lay patient advocates.

- *Tell the patient and family what happened and how:* "Caregivers should be honest and open about the incident and about what is being done to mitigate the injury and to prevent a recurrence. Honest communication conveys respect for the patient. Failure to acknowledge the event can be very distressing for the patient and is a powerful stimulus to complaint or litigation."
- *Take responsibility:* "As the person the patient entrusts their care to, the attending physician must assume responsibility even when he/she did not actually make the mistake that caused the injury."

- *Apologize:* "When there has been an error, one of the most powerful things a caregiver can do to heal the patient—and him/herself—is to apologize. ... Explaining the event, communicating remorse, and making a gesture of reconciliation can do much to defuse the hurt and anger that follows an injury."
- *Explain what will be done to prevent future events:* "Knowing that changes were made and that some good came of their experience helps the patient and family cope with their pain or loss."
- *I'll add one more:* **Be humble and always be a mensch.***

HANDLING ANGER

- Are you engaging in judgmental *should* thinking?
- Are you losing perspective?
- Are you personalizing?

---

* A mensch is "someone to admire and emulate, someone of noble character. The key to being 'a real mensch' is nothing less than character, rectitude, dignity, a sense of what is right, responsible, decorous." Rosten, Leo. 1968. The Joys of Yiddish. New York: Pocket Books. P. 237

CHAPTER 12
WHAT OTHERS SAY

AFTER READING THIS BOOK, YOU might be surprised to learn that other people have different ideas about and approaches to improving the patient experience. Shocking, no? Can you imagine two different architects coming up with different designs for an office building? Or two three-star Michelin chefs with two distinct ways to cook branzino? Or two eight-year-olds with different approaches to eating Oreos?

You can? Well, good. Then you'll be interested in what's to follow. In researching this book, I read widely on the patient experience and even, with credit, advocated others' ideas. But I want you to know about others' approaches for the simple reason that I realize, as I said way back in the Introduction, that not every technique and strategy in the book will appeal to every health professional. You should be able to pick and choose what will work for you with your particular personality and practice situation.

So here are some other people's takes on improving the patient experience along with some comments and the occasional snide aside.[*]

---

[*] One more thing. As of this writing I have no financial or other relationship with any of the organizations or people I mention, except as otherwise noted.

DR. ADAM SMITH

I MET ADAM AT AN author's retreat and immediately found many reasons to dislike him: young, very handsome, fit, smart, nice head of hair, gorgeous wife with a new baby on the way. You understand, right? Within five minutes of meeting him, it became apparent that Adam is such a fine physician and such a kind, caring, thoughtful human being that my preconceptions vanished, and we quickly became friends.

One of Adam's many medical roles is as a physician development coach at a large multispecialty clinic in Texas. He actually goes into the room with underperforming physicians and then reviews the patient encounter with them and suggests ways to improve it. I think Adam's ideas are excellent, and that is why I've put them first in this chapter.

He noticed that many of the doctors he worked with were "busying themselves with technology. Or they were wedded to a routine that was no longer, in my opinion, functional. So they were coming in and standing. Or they arrived, and before making physical or even eye contact to make some human connection, they just went to the computer and were logging in prior to acknowledging that there was a human in the room who was there with a need."

Adam found that doctors developed a routine for collecting information from patients about their symptoms—onset, duration, location, etc.—which didn't allow a story to be told. "We don't listen for the story. We kind of file it into those categories so we can communicate in a professional lingo that [to us] gets to the heart of the matter."

So Adam developed a script for doctors to use "as a foundation for yet another script or protocol that can be customized [so] there's room for improvisation and ownership that focuses on the connection but still allows them to incorporate their routine."

Adam has kindly granted me permission to include his script in this book. You'll find it in Appendix I, along with some of Adam's comments.

EMPATHETICS™

DR. HELEN RIESS, THE FOUNDER of Empathetics, is an Associate Professor of Psychiatry at Harvard Medical School and Director of the Empathy and Relational Science Program at Massachusetts General Hospital. She has done research into the neuroscience of empathy, and her company offers online courses as well as executive education, facilitated workshops, and individual coaching. Riess and her colleagues state on their website that they provide "innovative empathy and interpersonal skills training through eLearning for medical professionals leveraging new, scientifically proven methods that enhance human relationships and make medical practice more effective and efficient."

I've taken the Empathetics eLearning courses. They are *Introduction to the Neuroscience and Practice of Empathy, Managing Difficult Medical Interactions*, and *Delivering Bad News*. I found them to be excellent, with useful information any physician, nurse, or other health professional could apply to his or her work. My only complaint is that you have to watch the videos within a certain amount of time after you register and give Empathetics your money. I wanted to review the videos again before writing this chapter, but I would have had to pay all over again to watch. Dear Reader, my love for you does have limits.

Learn more at: www.Empathetics.com

LANGUAGE OF CARING©

THIS ORGANIZATION EMPHASIZES COMMUNICATION SKILL building and it works primarily with institutions. The principals are Wendy Leebov, EdD, Jill Gold, and Dorothy Sisneros, and they have a team of doctors, nurses, PhDs, and MBAs who work with hospitals and healthcare systems.

While their business is geared toward institutions, they have published a fine book for practitioners called *The Language of Caring Guide for Physicians: Communication Essentials for Patient-Centered Care* by Dr. Leebov and Dr. Carla Rotering. The book teaches several "competencies," including mindful practice, effective openings and closings, engaging patients and families as partners, communicating with empathy, and having hard conversations.

I found the book to be useful and dense with information. It includes suggested dialogue for physicians in the form of tips with suggested wordings, strategies for different situations, and checklists aplenty. I think it makes a fine reference book, but one which might be a little overwhelming to try to read straight through and absorb everything.

Their website is www.LanguageofCaring.com

ALAN ALDA

YES, THAT ALAN ALDA. As I was finishing the first draft of this book, I heard Mr. Alda interviewed on NPR about his new book, *If I Understood You, Would I Have This Look on My Face? My Adventures in the Art and Science of Relating and Communicating.*[1] I pulled my car over, took out my phone, and immediately ordered the book.

An actor by trade and a Renaissance man by nature, Mr. Alda helped establish the Center for Communicating Science at Stony Brook University, which is a half-hour drive from my house—if you speed a little.

The book is about "developing empathy and learning to recognize what the other person is thinking," two essential skills for doctors. Mr. Alda states that much of what he has learned about communication "stems from the experience of standing face-to-face on stage with another actor... And it can be learned by anyone, not just those touched with a talent for acting."

You can understand, I hope, why Mr. Alda's approach resonates so deeply with me. Performance techniques to improve communication. Or the patient experience. He is another performer with similar ideas. A kindred spirit.*

In any event, I recommend Mr. Alda's book as the next book you should read after this one.

MICHAEL PORT†

AND THE BOOK TO READ after that is *Steal the Show* by Michael Port.[2] This book shows how performance is part of many aspects of our lives, even if we don't realize it. Port is an actor who trained at the NYU Graduate Acting Program and became one of the top public speakers in the country. This is a highly readable, comprehensive, and practical treatise that will show you how to "perform" in any situation from, as the subtitle says, "speeches to job interviews to deal-closing pitches." If you ever have to teach students or residents, present at grand rounds, address a group of colleagues, or lecture your kids, this book will be an immense help.

DR. ROBIN YOUNGSON

DR. YOUNGSON IS AN ANESTHESIOLOGIST from New Zealand who promotes "human-centered healthcare" through his organization Hearts in Healthcare. I particularly like his book *Time to Care*, which is a compassionate examination of not only the patient experience, but also the physician's. His opening chapter is called "Burnout," which shows you the importance he places on caring for the physician.

The book is full of advice and good practices for physicians to help show empathy, to make us both more compassionate and more efficient

---

* Though I'm not so hubristic as to think that I should be in the same room as Mr. Alda, much less the same category. He's Alan Alda; I'm a *pisher*.
† Michael and his wife Amy have since become my friends and mentors.

in our work, and to help us enjoy practicing. Here are a few of my favorite quotes:

Many of us are practiced in the art of conveying busyness. The quick movements, brisk attention to clinical tasks, lack of eye contact, and clipped speech all portray a powerful message: I'm here for you in a strictly limited role, I'm not going to connect with you, and I don't have time for questions or concerns. The manner in which we reveal our mental state and attitudes are almost completely nonverbal—our facial expressions, tone of voice, eye contact, and body language. This means that we have all the time in the world to convey an attitude of care, kindness and compassion even when we are busy performing clinical tasks.[3]

Collect yourself before you meet your next patient. 'Collecting yourself' literally means pulling together the pieces. When over-busy, our attention becomes fragmented among competing demands. Pause, take a breath and think about your attitude. Are you going to bring softness, kindness and openhearted compassion into the room or else project an attitude of ill humor and busyness? It's amazing how many health workers are grumpy with their patients."[4]

Tiny acts of loving-kindness are the bedrock of happy and fulfilling practice. Researchers in positive psychology have shown there is no more powerful way to begin to increase your stores of positivity and happiness. The habit of kindness will enhance and strengthen all the parts of the brain concerned with loving kindness empathy, no-judgment and pro-social behavior [sentence order of excerpt modified for clarity].[5]

Much of Dr. Youngson's advice is close to my heart. His book is not preachy, and I highly recommend it. *Time for Caring* is available from your favorite monopolistic online store.

Here are works of other authors that you may find of interest:

Scott Louis Diering, MD

Dr. Diering's book is entitled *Love Your Patients! Improving Patient Satisfaction with Essential Behaviors That Enrich the Lives of Patients & Professionals.*[6] I would recommend this for the more spiritually inclined reader.

Dr. Diering's thesis and emphasis is that we need to approach our patients with *agape* love.[*] This he describes as "the deep spiritual love, the love of empathy and understanding, the love of openness and interest, the love of caring and compassion [that] everyone needs to feel, *especially* our patients." There are also practical suggestions similar to some that I've given you.

A good part of the book is devoted to stories, horror stories really, about patients being treated poorly by doctors, nurses, and other medical personnel. Then the author asks the same questions about the behaviors of the medical personnel: "Where is the love?" "Where is the compassion?" "Where is the respect?" I wanted to ask, "Where is the subtlety?"

I am certain that Dr. Diering is a warm, compassionate, and passionate physician. That comes through loud and clear in his book. The lessons he teaches and the points he makes are important and worthy. His approach did not, however, resonate with me. It might with you.

Thomas H. Lee, MD

Dr. Lee is the Chief Medical Officer of Press Ganey, the country's leading creator of patient satisfaction surveys, serving over 40 percent of the hospitals and health systems in the country. His book, *An Epidemic of Empathy in Healthcare: How to Deliver Compassionate, Connected*

---

[*] At first your humble, somewhat slow author did not realize the pronunciation is ah-gah'-peh. I thought the goal was to love patients so much that we left their mouths agape. Oy.

Patient Care That Creates a Competitive Advantage,[7] is a call for making empathy as important as science in health care, surely a worthy goal.

Dr. Lee is certainly a "thought leader"* in health care these days, and this is a serious, well-researched work. The book is intended more for department chairs and hospital administrators and less for the everyday practitioner. For instance, nearly a fifth of the book is devoted to the measurement of patient experience and satisfaction—not surprising considering that's his company's business. The information is interesting for, but not applicable to, daily practice.

JACQUELYN SMALL WITH JIM MULRY, MD

Ms. Small is a therapist and educator with a master's in social work and the author of nine books on personal growth. Her collaborator, Dr. Mulry, is a family practitioner with certification in "addictionology, medical acupuncture, and The Eupsychia Process of Psychospiritual Integration and Integrative Breathwork." Their book, *Improving Your Bedside Manner: A Handbook for Physicians to Develop Therapeutic Conversations with Their Patients*,[8] is a concise, 120-page treatise on how to enhance in yourself "ten personality variables that determine high effectiveness as a therapeutic person in the life of another."

The characteristics are Empathy, Genuineness, Respect, Self-disclosure, Warmth, Immediacy, Concreteness, Therapeutic Confrontation, Potency, and Self-actualization. In each chapter, the authors define the personality trait, give examples of doctor-patient conversations that show the trait in action, and warn of "toxic responses" from physicians that will, unfortunately, sound familiar to many of us. The authors then give guidance for physician self-reflection on each trait.

---

* To understand what a thought leader is, watch this: https://www.youtube.com/watch?v=_ZBKX-6Gz6A

This book seeks to help you become a better you by enhancing strengths you already have and thus become a better physician for your patients. The author states her hope that the book "has enabled you to see yourself on every page with utter self-honesty."

You know where to buy it online.

JAMES MERLINO, MD

In contrast, Dr. Merlino's dense, small print, 245-page book is designed as an experiential guide for large health care systems. It's called *Service Fanatics: How to Build Superior Patient Experience the Cleveland Clinic Way.*[9] Dr. Merlino was, after all, the Chief Experience Officer of that organization. The book is about how to change the culture of an institution to make it patient-centered and all the struggles the Cleveland Clinic endured to make itself a leader in patient customer satisfaction. Most valuable to individual practitioners would be Chapters 10 and 11, "Healthcare Requires Service Excellence" and "Doctors Need to Communicate Better." Otherwise, the book is for the C-suite folks.

STEPHEN C. BEESON, MD

Dr. Beeson is another physician leader interested in helping organizations such as health systems and medical practices achieve excellence, and his book *Practicing Excellence: A Physician's Manual to Exceptional Health Care*[10] is a detailed prescriptive for doing just that. You will find it especially useful if you are charged with improving your group's performance. His basic thesis is stated at the outset: "Medical care, workplace conditions, clinical quality, service, and the culture of a medical organization will ultimately be determined by the conduct of its physicians." It's hard to argue with that.

There are two chapters with specific recommendations for the patient encounter that would be of particular interest to clinicians: Chapter 3, "Physician Service Excellence Tools," and Chapter 11, "Physician Best Practices."

As you can see from this brief survey, books about the patient experience fall into two broad categories: books about improving institutions and books about improving you. Some of the latter I found to be preachy. Alan Alda's and Michael Port's books are the most fun to read.

CHAPTER 13
CURTAIN

DID I LOVE GOING TO work every day? Nope. There were lousy days, annoying patients, and non-patient stresses: staff not performing as I would've liked, disagreements with partners, doctors who left the practice, an attempt by a hospital workers union to unionize our private office, bad financial years, managed care, patient surveys, online reviews, and four malpractice suits.[*]

One day in the mid-1990s, I was driving my wife and kids to visit her family in New Jersey. I was not in a good mood. First of all, it had been a hard week in the office: late hours and one night spent in the ICU with a GI bleeder. Second, we were going to visit the in-laws, whom I loved dearly, but you know... And, third, Jersey!

We were cruising down the New Jersey Turnpike when we passed a billboard advertising one of the new managed care plans. This was when managed care was first coming in, and it was a difficult and confusing time for doctors. I hated what [mis]managed care was doing to medicine. So, being tired and cranky, seeing that sign set me off. I started to rant about all the things that were frustrating me about being a doctor.

---

[*] One (post-flexible sigmoidoscopy chemical colitis) was settled for a small amount, two were dismissed, and one I was dropped from. But they all hurt.

"I hate this managed care stuff*! The insurance companies are trying to control how I practice; they don't care about what's best for my patients! And my malpractice premiums are soaring, so every day I go to work feeling like lawyers are looking over my shoulder, waiting to pounce if I make a mistake. And on top of everything else, I'm working much harder to make less money!"

At that moment, my fifteen-year-old daughter in the back seat, Danielle, looked up from her book and said, "You know, Daddy, you have a crappy job."

From the mouths of babes, right?

At times, it did feel like a crappy job. But most of the time, patient visits felt great. There was a natural high that came from doing my best for another human being that was like the high of a great performance. It was some time, though, before I made the connection between performing and seeing patients. It took the tragedy of a little girl with lissencephaly to make me conscious of the link.

As I mentioned in Chapter 2, if you have ever been a performer of any type—actor, musician, dancer, athlete, mime, juggler, teacher, lawyer, even ventriloquist—you know how great you feel after a good performance that really connects with an audience. All your efforts and practice have come to fruition. You've brought excitement and pleasure into the lives of others. You may have even exceeded your own expectations. On top of all that, performing releases endorphins.[1]

I suspect that a good performance with a patient does, too. Yes, there is the deep intellectual satisfaction of applying our years of study and training to solve a medical problem. There is the justifiable pride in using painstakingly acquired manual dexterity to repair a human body. But there is intellectual satisfaction in computer coding and pride in the manual dexterity needed to carve a beautiful piece of furniture. What's missing in those, which both performing and medicine have in abundance, is the human connection.

---

* Not the actual word I used.

It is the human connection that we can achieve by treating every patient encounter as a performance. By applying the techniques and strategies of the stage—listening and observing, responding in the moment, staying in character, acting as if, and breathing—we can connect more deeply with our patients, make ourselves the actual therapeutic instrument, and create the ideal patient experience. That feels really, really good. And makes practicing medicine a joy.

That's why all those years ago I had an epiphany on the New Jersey Turnpike. I said to my daughter, "Actually, Danielle, when I think about it, I have a really great job, and I'll tell you why. When I go to work every day, there's only one thing that I have to do: Perform my best for that one person in the room with me. I don't have to outsmart someone in a court of law. I don't have to try to convince someone to buy something. I don't have to live or die by the Dow Jones index.

"And at the end of the day, I won't have manufactured the most widgets or moved the most product, and I certainly will not have made the most money. But there will be thousands and thousands of people whose lives will be better because they met me, and that's the best job in the world."

Who else gets to do what we doctors and other health professionals do? To contribute in the most intimate way to other people's lives. To have them understand innately that their betterment is our sole concern. To be trusted with their single most valuable possession, their health. To dedicate our minds, our eyes, our ears, our hands, and our hearts to helping other people. And so to save the world, one life at a time.

All it takes, every time we walk into that room, is for us to give the performance of a lifetime.

APPENDICES

COLLECTED TAKEAWAYS

CHAPTER 1
OUR CHANGING MEDICAL WORLD

- The practice of medicine is undergoing the most radical changes of our lifetimes.
- Doctors face a loss of income, autonomy, and respect.
- Many physicians are unhappy with their choice of profession.
- As fee-for-service vanishes, quality and patient experience will come to the fore.
- The only thing we can directly control is the patient encounter.

CHAPTER 2
THE PATIENT VISIT IS A PERFORMANCE

- In our lives, we have many selves, perform many roles.
- When we see patients, we are being the biggest, best version of our physician selves.
- Good performance is authentic behavior in a manufactured environment.
- We want to create genuine emotions in our patients.
- A good performance enhances empathy.
- A performance is enjoyable.
- Making your visit a performance satisfies patients.

CHAPTER 3
I'M NOT A PERFORMER AND DON'T WANT TO BE

- You don't have to be a performer to give a good performance.
- You can try the techniques in this book without consciously thinking you're performing.
- Successful businesses use the "performance" model to give great customer service.
- Ventriloquists are cool.

CHAPTER 4
WHAT PATIENTS WANT

- Patients want us to listen to them.
- They want us to respect them.
- They want us to know them.
- They want us to give them enough time.

CHAPTER 5
THE FIVE BASIC PERFORMANCE TECHNIQUES WE NEED

- We are using performance techniques to enhance our authentic behavior.
- True listening also requires attention to facial expressions and body language.
- Our assumptions about patients can affect our observations of them.
- Reacting is a reflex; responding is a choice.
- Being in the moment benefits both patients and us.
- Staying in the moment helps us stay in character—our doctor selves.
- Acting as if can get us through difficult days.

- Breathing cyclically with mouth slightly open makes us more relatable.
- Using all these techniques together enhances our empathy.

CHAPTER 6
SETTING THE STAGE: WHAT TO DO BEFORE YOU GO IN WITH THE PATIENT

NINETY-SIX PERCENT OF PATIENT COMPLAINTS are about the customer service, not the doctors.

THE VENUE
- Is it easy for patients to get to and park?
- What impression does the decor give?
- Is the office warm and welcoming?
- Is it kept neat and clean? Any brooms in the corner?

SUPPORTING CAST
- Remember that staff are dealing with patients at their worst.
- Their "customer service" job is much harder than ours.
- The doctors set the tone of the office.
- Kindness and respect toward staff will result in kindness and respect toward patients.
- How would you want your mother to be treated?

AUDIENCE MANAGEMENT
- The doctor or medical assistant should keep the front staff informed as to how far behind the doctor is running.
- Patients should be informed truthfully about wait times.
- Productively occupy patients' time and "get them started" with a simple questionnaire in which they list their three principal concerns for today's visit.
- Offer free Wi-Fi.

- Make sure there are no unexplained waits.
- Go into the waiting room yourself to explain a delay to a patient; all the others will take note.
- Overestimate the wait time.
- Be sure of a good ending to the wait.

A DOCTOR PREPARES

- Review the chart before you go in with the patient: at least the problem list and the last visit.
- Review "personal tidbits" the patient has told you previously and bring them up at the very outset of the visit.

MAKING YOUR ENTRANCE

- Take a breath and collect yourself outside the exam room door. You are preparing to be in the moment and getting in character.
- Smile. Act as if you are about to see a good friend you haven't seen for years, and that warm Duchenne smile will naturally come out.

CHAPTER 7
IN THE ROOM WITH THE PATIENT

THE GREETING

- Enter the room genuinely glad to see the patient; it is a privilege to do this work.
- Choose the familiarness- and age-appropriate greeting.
- Use a neutral or "welcoming" handshake that conveys warmth and trust.
- Tell the patient how you like to be addressed; ask his preference.

SIT OR STAND? AND WHERE?

- Sit during the visit to give the perception of spending more time.

- In the consulting office, sit at the same corner of the desk as the patient.
- Be careful of the positioning of your feet.
- In the exam room, sit at or below the patient's eye level.

GETTING DOWN TO BUSINESS
- Remember who's the boss. Be humble.
- Start the conversation with knowledge: personal tidbits or medical.
- Keep your tone of voice warm, not dominant.

EYE CONTACT AND CONVEYING EMPATHY
- Use the "social gaze," making eye contact 60 to 70 percent of the time.
- Do the triple nod to show active listening.
- Tilt your head to your active listening side during the triple nod to convey empathy.
- Reflect back to the patient important or emotional content.

INTERRUPTIONS AND EXPECTATIONS
- Let the patient speak; don't interrupt in twelve to eighteen seconds.
- Accentuate the positive.

THE DAMNED COMPUTER
- Don't let the computer get between you and the patient:
- Alternate your attention between the two or
- Use a primitive analog device.

THE PHYSICAL EXAM
- Narrate the physical.

EXITING
- Ask, "Does our plan sound reasonable to you?"
- Ask, "Are there any other questions you want to ask or concerns you want to bring to my attention before I go?"
- End the visit with a gentle touch.

THE ROLE OF HUMOR
- Use humor, if you know how.
- Or else I *will* send those puppets.

FINALLY
- Remember, the performance is not over.

CHAPTER 8
THE PERFORMANCE MUST GO ON

- Keep your promises.
- Under-promise. Over-deliver.
- Manage expectations proactively.
- Provide moments of patient astonishment.
- Consider asking patients to write online reviews.
- Learn from negative ones. Let the patients see you've learned.
- Explain to patients how surveys work.
- Ask them to give you "the highest rating you think I deserve."
- Play God when necessary.
- At your own risk.

CHAPTER 9
MORE TECHNIQUES TO TRY: IMPROVISATION AND STORYTELLING

- Improv is a valuable skill in medicine and in life.
- "Yes, and…" is more effective than "Yes, but…"

- Stories and analogies are powerful tools to help connect with patients
- Contribute your stories and analogies to the Story Bank.

CHAPTER 10
PUTTING IT ALL TO WORK

- Forming new habits takes time, an average of sixty-six days.
- Reinstitute techniques you've read about here but are out of the habit of doing.
- Choose a few new techniques and strategies and work on using them every day.
- Add new ones every few weeks to months.
- Make a mental note of how patients are reacting to you. Do you notice a difference?
- Remember, it's a performance!
- Keep your patient visit performance fresh by listening and responding.
- Every audience, and patient, is different.
- The work we do is a privilege.

CHAPTER 11
WHEN THINGS GO WRONG

DISASTERS
- Tell the patient what happened and how.
- Take responsibility.
- Apologize.
- Explain what will happen to prevent future events.

HANDLING ANGER
- Are you engaging in judgmental *should* thinking?
- Are you losing perspective?

- Are you personalizing?

CHAPTER 12
WHAT OTHERS SAY

- Read Alan Alda's *If I Understood You, Would I Have This Look on My Face?*
- Read Michael Port's *Steal the Show.*
- The other books are purely elective.

CHAPTER 13
CURTAIN

- We have the best job in the world.
- With every patient visit, give the performance of a lifetime.

APPENDIX I
DR. ADAM SMITH'S SCRIPT

The Clinical Script

Build trust and rapport. Educate and accommodate (as best you are able and within reason).

1. Entrance: Establish rapport.
   - Knock before entering.
   - Enter the room and greet the patient while foaming hands and stethoscope [with disinfectant].
   - Greet the patient by name. Introduce yourself and welcome the patient.
   - Intro suggestion: "Hello, Mr. Jones. I'm Dr. Smith. Welcome. I see that the team collected a strep swab. I've briefly reviewed your chart and I'd like to hear a little more from you about what brought you in today."

Adam adds: I encourage doctors to acknowledge any testing that's been done before they arrived. For instance, many clinics can do a strep or a flu test or a urinalysis. Often I've got that information before I go in. I don't want to say, "So, what brings you in today?" because, if they're having a really bad day, they think, "Oh, God, I've got to tell this whole story all over again," or, "Oh, God, this doctor doesn't even know why I'm here."

2. HPI: Listen to their story.
   • Listen to all of it.
   • Paraphrase what they've told you to ensure you understand their story and so they can hear it back.
   • You can paraphrase as you go, requesting more information as needed. For example: "So the sore throat began two nights ago, followed by some cough and congestion. Any other symptoms that are bothering you or keeping you up at night?"
   • Ask about interventions they may have tried at home. For instance: "Is there anything you've tried so far that you've found helpful or not so helpful?"

Adam adds: The second stage or phase of the script invites open-ended questions and asks the patient for permission to investigate things further. "Would you mind telling me a little bit more about that?" Paraphrasing is very important in my approach. They might say, "My throat hurts." I answer, "I understand that your throat's really painful, and we'll talk more about that. Would you mind sharing with me a few other details like when it started and any other symptoms such as fever?

Without the support of that script, I've observed physicians getting instantly frustrated, and taking a position like: "This patient has no idea how to tell the story, and now I'm going to have to barrage them with twenty-two bullet-point, yes-or-no questions." That would leave the patient feeling interrogated rather than heard, and so I encourage the physicians to paraphrase and inquire until they can actually summarize the story for themselves.

3. Exam & ROS
   • Invite them to the exam table. In general, ask permission as you go.
   • While performing the exam, ask any additional systems-related questions that may arise. While looking in the ears, you might inquire about headache, for example.

- Remember always to honor the patient's experience. How they feel is real, regardless of our findings. Make the opportunity to validate their experience in case of negative exam findings. "Your throat looks okay, understanding that it doesn't feel okay."

Adam adds: Inviting patients keeps them in the driver's seat, so that they are always in control of the visit. It creates the environment and it's not a façade. It's true. You're asking, you're giving, you're inviting them, they always have the opportunity to say no. They're in charge.

I encourage doctors to incorporate their review of systems into the examination rather than building it into bullet-points during the interview. It's time effective, time efficient, and it keeps you engaged with the patient so you're not doing the examination *to* the patient, you're doing it *with the patient.*

4. Return to the desk. Invite the patient to return to the couch or chair.
   - Share your impression and suggestions for treatment or another symptom-focused actionable plan.
   - Remember: Just because you don't have a diagnosis doesn't mean you can't make a plan.
   - Invite their participation: "Does that sound like a reasonable plan to you?"
   - Continue: "Is there anything else that you wanted to cover related to your throat that we haven't addressed?"

5. Set expectations and frame the end of the visit.
   - For example, you might say: "Next, the MA/nurse is going to come back and check you out from the room, and, in the meantime I'll send over your prescriptions (or, complete your paperwork, order bloodwork, etc.) and we'll have you on your way shortly."

- In closing, ask, "Do you have any questions before I go?" This ensures that the visit is concluded on a patient-centered note and provides the opportunity to relate back to what's most important to the patient.
- Thank the patient. "Thank you for coming in."
- Conclude the session and exit the room.

REMINDERS AND PRINCIPLES TO GUIDE EACH VISIT

- Remember that you don't know what the patient's life is like. Give everyone the benefit of the doubt.
- You don't have to take things personally
- You don't have to be responsible for everything

To which I, Bob, would add: I think those are pretty good guiding principles for life.

APPENDIX II
CHARLES "BUCK" ADAMS ON BODY LANGUAGE

CHARLES "BUCK" ADAMS IS A retired Alaska undercover narcotics detective, now a widely respected financial adviser, and also a certified body language expert and Instant Influence trainer. He is also, after my brother, my favorite Republican. Here, in Buck's own words, is additional information we physicians can use with our patients:

My interest in nonverbal communication began as a child. Being an Army brat, constantly on the move across the country, repeatedly made me the new kid on the block and forced me to quickly figure out how to distinguish friend from foe. After college, I became a police officer and spent the next twenty years in law enforcement. A police officer's survival depends on being constantly aware of the nonverbal cues of those around him and especially being on the alert for signs of threat or deception. Three of those twenty years, I worked deep undercover as a narcotics investigator. Drug dealers have a nasty habit of pointing guns at you while searching you for weapons or, worse, a wire. I was usually unarmed and with no means of communicating with other investigators. Paying close attention to whether or not a dealer was buying the story I was telling was literally a matter of life and death.

A basic observation: More than four decades of experience, whether on the streets as a police officer or sitting across from hundreds of clients in high-stakes financial situations, has taught me that body language is a two-way communication: while paying close attention to the nonverbal cues of others is important, it is *equally—if not more—important that we are also in tune with the nonverbal signals we ourselves are constantly broadcasting.* We have within us the power to quickly change the entire dynamic of an interaction simply by being aware of the types of nonverbal cues we are emitting and making subtle and simple changes. A significant body of research has shown that over 60 percent of the actual or interpreted meaning of a message is conveyed through nonverbal communication signals!

HANDSHAKE

The handshake carries tremendous power, especially in Western culture. Extensive cross-cultural research reveals that even in cultures for whom the handshake is not the traditional greeting, visible—and preferably open—hands are the universal, initial, primary trust indicators. Judging by activity in the limbic system, the most ancient area of our brain, the hands are the first thing we note when someone approaches us, whether we are aware of it or not. It is hardwired into our psyches to immediately evaluate if someone presents a threat to us when we first meet them.

Long before the science of body language became mainstream, we were taught as rookie police officers to "Watch the hands; that's where death is dealt."

There are three broad categories of handshake: dominant, submissive, and neutral.

Dominant: The dominant handshake is to be used with great care, as it transmits several powerful subconscious signals to the person receiving it and is rarely, rarely appropriate! A dominant handshake consists of twisting the recipient's hand into a palm-up position, exposing the underside of their wrist and forearm. Immediately, the receiver of such a handshake has both lost physical leverage and had the very vulnerable anterior side of their wrist and forearm exposed.

A dominant handshake immediately triggers a limbic response of feeling exposed and at risk. Also, unless someone approaches you with their palm already facing up, the dominant handshake requires more force to be applied when the receiver's wrist is twisted palm up. This sends a clear message of an attempt to appear dominant. Bottom line, it probably shouldn't even be in your inventory. If this is the way you currently shake hands, stop!

Another dominant tendency that many politicians have is to use what is referred to as the "politician's handshake". This is a double-clasp handshake using two hands to grasp one of the other person's and is an effort to create immediate intimacy. However, it is the equivalent of a hug, as it momentarily *traps* the other person's hand. Politicians may shake tens of thousands of hands during a campaign. There is always someone—an overenthusiastic supporter, a foe in the crowd, or just a random someone—who likes to apply a crushing handshake. The double-clasp gives the politician the ability to hold the top of the other person's hand and wrist and pull their right hand free if necessary. If you already know someone well, and they would be just as comfortable giving or receiving a hug from you or this is the way they like to greet you, then go ahead and have at it. Otherwise, leave it behind.

Submissive: In contrast, and depending on your goal, if you want to transmit to someone that they have a measure of control and some power in a situation, approaching them with your palm partially up allows them to deliver a dominant handshake to you, usually without any conscious recognition of the act and without their needing to exert force. In doing so, you are sending a limbic signal that you feel comfortable enough in the situation to expose your own wrist. As Dr. Baker mentions in Chapter 7, he frequently used this handshake to give patients some sense of control in an environment where they may understandably be feeling that they have little control. I often use a partial palm-up handshake myself when a new client comes in and I want to help them relax.

Neutral: The neutral handshake is the most common, and frankly the *safest*, handshake to use. Dry, vertical, and with matching pressure are the components of the preferred handshake, suitable in almost all situations. Matching the pressure received is preferred.

(Sidebar: Men, we are often guilty of assuming a very strong handshake is the way to go. Bear in mind, what might be considered a strong handshake between men can be painful to someone else, especially to women, as they tend to wear more rings than men.)

HANDSHAKE TIPS AND TECHNIQUES

Beyond the basics of a neutral handshake, there are ways to improve your technique even further.

Left foot lead: In general, most people, as they approach one another to shake hands, tend to lean forward with the upper body and lead with their *right* foot as they extend their right hand. This keeps both party's bodies farther apart, maintaining a "safe" distance. If your goal is to help someone become comfortable quickly, try the following variant.

As you reach to shake someone's hand, lead slightly with your left foot rather than your right. If you don't already do this, it may take a bit of practice to learn to do this automatically, but it pays big dividends. First, it brings your stomach closer to the other person's hand, subconsciously signaling that you're comfortable and trusting enough to allow you to have the other person's hand close to your unprotected and exposed abdominal area. This sends a powerful nonverbal trust cue. At the same time, it allows you to easily reach forward with your left hand and apply a gentle and brief touch to the other person's elbow, creating another point of contact.

In American culture, the area between the forearm and elbow is generally considered a "social space" where brief contact between newly introduced people is permissible. My preference is about a one-second touch of the right elbow, or the forearm if it's more convenient. Above the elbow, you begin to move into areas many people consider private space and are uncomfortable being touched. Stay away from the triceps with a new contact. Most men and women don't appreciate your checking out the size or firmness of their triceps. Alpha types who like to pull close people with whom they are not well-acquainted and grasp their shoulder or triceps are, at a limbic level, exerting dominance, not equality.

Note: As with all things, there are exceptions. As an example, if you happen to be 6'4" approaching someone 5'2", stepping too close can intimidate the other person, despite your best intentions. Use your best judgment. All things in moderation.

Proxemics (distance): After you finish shaking the hand, step back and let the other party set the distance from you where *they* are comfortable standing. This comfortable "social distance" differs not only by culture and country, but also regionally within the same country. It's always better to afford the other person the opportunity to set the distance they are comfortable with. In the United States, a distance of zero to eighteen inches is considered intimate space. One-and-a-half to five feet is personal space. Five to seven feet between people is their social space, and beyond seven feet, public. These distances do not make up a hard and fast rule, just a guideline. As our society continues to become more culturally diverse, these distances may well evolve.

The Feet: The feet are considered by most body language experts to be the most truthful part of the body. That may sound strange, but consider this. We are trained from a very early age to control our facial expressions. "Smile at your Aunt Helen," "Don't make that face around me," etc. The farther we move away from the face, the more likely we are to see truthful, albeit unconscious, behavior. When movements of the feet express emotions that are incongruent with what's being said, or expressed on someone's face, believe the feet. We rarely pay attention to what our feet are doing, even though our feet have always been our primary method of locomotion to get us out of trouble. When you can see someone's feet, you have the opportunity to see:

a. Apprehension: locking ankles around a chair leg, pulling feet underneath them, crossing ankles tightly. The feet are trying to retreat despite the smile on a person's face.

b. Flight: A very common position people assume when they are ready to leave or feel threatened is what is referred to as "the runner's stance." This consists of one foot pulled back under the chair while the other is pushed out in front of the chair. Usually, one or both hands are also on the knees. Picture a sprinter on the starting blocks. A second version of the flight position is when someone's foot points toward the exit while they are still engaged with you. I have practiced avoiding assuming this position for years and will still catch myself cocking a foot toward the door or away from a group I might be standing with when I'm ready to go. Most fascinating, I may not yet even be consciously aware that I want to move on. And yet I am likely sending a subconscious signal to the other party that I am ready to leave.

APPENDIX III
NORMAN KANTER, PHD ON HANDLING ANGER

Author: How can physicians use cognitive psychology to help them deal with patients who make us angry?

Dr. Kanter: What I'm going to present to you is right from cognitive therapy. It is a synthesis that my friend Dr. Dennis Gallo [of Commack, NY] made from the original work of two of the founders of cognitive psychology, Dr. Aaron Beck and Dr. Albert Ellis.

What physicians need to know is that the negative emotions that they have—whether they be anxiety, depression, frustration, embarrassment, guilt, or irritability—these negative emotions always come from the thoughts that we have. This is the essence of cognitive therapy. Whenever we are experiencing any intense negative emotion, it really is coming from errors in thinking.

In order to see this concept, you need to be aware that there is a model, an ABC model, which is right from cognitive therapy. *A* would represent a situation and *C* would represent an emotion. It's not *A*, the situation, that's triggering the emotion, but rather point *B*, the all-important thinking reaction. We have thoughts going on all the time, even when we're not aware of them. Sometimes it's difficult to catch the thoughts that are going on, but as we become more skilled at it, like any skill, it becomes easier to catch thoughts.

Author: Can you give me some examples of thoughts going on that we're not aware of?

Dr. Kanter: Okay. Let's say that I'm speaking to you in my office and a stranger barges in and points a gun at me. I would immediately feel, let's say, an anxiety level of ninety-five to one hundred on a scale of zero to one hundred. I wouldn't be aware of any thoughts that would be going on, but there would be thoughts going on, and they would be split-second thoughts like, "Oh, my God, there's a stranger, what does he want? Is he going to kill me? Is he going to hurt me? How did this happen? Why didn't I just lock the door, and what an idiot I am that I didn't safeguard my own safety!" All these thoughts, a whole paragraph of thoughts, are going on without even my realizing it.

Author: Got it.

Dr. Kanter: I'll give you another example; it's slightly different. Let's say again I'm in my office and I'm looking at a piece of furniture, which is green. I'm looking at it, and it reminds me of green grass, and that reminds me of parks, and that reminds me of children playing in parks, and that reminds me of childhood, and that reminds me of my childhood, and that reminds me of Chicago, where I grew up, and that reminds me of my family, and that reminds me of my sister, and that reminds me of a phone call that I had with my sister that made me anxious. Now I'm looking at the green couch…

Author: And feeling anxious.

Dr. Kanter: I have no idea why I suddenly feel anxious. That feeling of anxiety is being triggered by my own thoughts.

Author: Right.

Dr. Kanter: Now, going more into the meat of this conversation, again, we're going to use an ABC model where *A* represents a situation, *C* represents a feeling, *B* is the all-important thinking reaction. At point *B*, there are three errors of thinking that we make, and if we're aware of them and we learn to catch them, we can decrease our negative emotions. That's the essence of what this conversation is about.

One of the errors we're going to call *should* thinking. Thinking with the word *should* in it is generally judgmental thinking. Instead, we want to strive for nonjudgmental thinking toward ourselves and toward other people. *Should* thinking raises the significance of something in our minds. *Should* thinking would be, "that patient should not have asked me an additional question, that patient should not have rolled their eyes, that patient should not have done X, Y, and Z." We need to correct that in our minds, because we have very limited control over what other people say and do. We have the ultimate control over how intensely we respond, but very little control over other people.

Author: Mm-hmm (affirmative).

Dr. Kanter: Whenever we find ourselves making the *should* error, which is very frequent for all of us, we are exaggerating the significance of the situation and we are going into negative judgmental thinking. Now, there is one form of the word *should* which is okay. It's when we use the word *should* in a nonjudgmental way. A nonjudgmental *should* would be something like this: "For little Johnny who's seven years old to learn to become a good student later on, he should do his homework now." There's no judgment there, it's just saying, "Hey, you want this skill to be developed later on, you ought to be doing such and such now." It's not saying little Johnny should do this or he's a bad person or little Johnny should do X, Y, and Z or he's bad. That would be negative judgmental *should* thinking.

Author: Sure.

Dr. Kanter: Once again, when a patient behaves in a way that we don't want, and this can be during the visit, or even anticipating what a difficult patient is going to be like, we want to catch and get rid of our *should* thinking and simply change it to *non-should* thinking. "There's no reason why this patient should behave in the way that *I* think they should."

The second error is losing perspective, making something huge out of something small. It's really similar to the philosophy of "don't sweat the small stuff," and it's all small stuff. We can use a scale from zero to one hundred in two ways. We can use it to measure the intensity of my anxiety or my depression or my irritability : I'm at a ninety in terms of irritability or I'm at an eighty in terms of anxiety. I'm at a sixty in terms of frustration. Or, we can use the scale in a different way to measure the objective horribleness of some event. On this scale from zero to one hundred of horribleness, we would reserve one hundred for things like death and dying for most people. One of the worst things imaginable would be, God forbid, the kidnapping of a child. That would be one hundred.

Author: Oh, yes.

Dr. Kanter: On that scale, most of the things that we face on a daily basis are certainly under twenty. On that scale, an eighty might be: I'm in a car accident and I'm partially paralyzed. Yet many of us will respond to daily situations like a difficult patient as seventy, eighty, ninety, one hundred, and how could that be? Well, we're losing perspective and we're forgetting at that moment all the things that would be really terrible. We're not including all the lesser things that ought to come into our picture. I'll give you an example.

To do that, I'm going to introduce one other concept. It's the concept of objective consequences, and this is also from Dennis Gallo. Let's say I am driving on the expressway, and a car cuts me off, and I go immediately to a ninety or one hundred in terms of anger, anxiety, frustration. What are the objective consequences of what just took place? Well, I slammed on my brakes, the cars never touched, we're all okay, and so, what are the objective consequences? I used up a micron of brake padding, and my body moved forward in space for a foot or so and then back again, but nothing else happened. In terms of objective consequences, that would be like two or five on a one hundred-point scale. So how could I be at a ninety-five emotionally? Well, there must be errors going on like losing perspective.

Author: Right.

Dr. Kanter: So when we get angry talking to a difficult, demanding, annoying patient, we are losing perspective in terms of how horrible that is compared to things that could really be horrible.

So far we've got two errors: *shoulding* and losing perspective.

Now the third and last error is probably the most difficult and the most common. We're going to call it personalizing. There are two kinds of personalizing. The first kind is when we take something too personally, too offensively, too sensitively, where we're affronted too easily. That's the first kind of personalizing. That's the one most likely to affect doctors as they're seeing patients.

An example might be when the patient says, "I told you that already, aren't you listening?" and we immediately go to a ninety. That's because we're taking it as a personal affront rather than realizing that the patient is so upset they're losing their manners.

The second kind of personalizing is the harder one to deal with. That is when we create a negative image of ourselves. One kind of thought would be, "If I don't have that person's approval, or everyone's approval, right now or all the time, I am not okay."

Another common thought is, "If I'm not doing something perfectly, I am not okay." Most of the personalizing that physicians do would be the first kind. However, if, for example, a patient questions us, and we get tongue-tied or can't come up with the answer immediately, we start to question our own ability and worth. That would be the second kind of personalizing, going into a negative image of self.

Now this sounds very simplistic: *shoulding*, losing perspective, personalizing. But these errors are sort of like DNA, in which there are just a few nucleic acids, but they can make infinite combinations. These are just three errors of thinking, but they are responsible for most of the negative emotions that we have.

We want to say to ourselves, when we're examining a patient or before or after, if I am emotionally over, say, twenty on a one hundred-point scale in any of these negative emotions, then I am probably *shoulding* and/or losing perspective and/or personalizing. Sometimes it's one, sometimes it's two, sometimes it's all three.

Now, Drs. Beck and Ellis actually outlined twelve or fifteen errors of thinking, but these three probably account for 90 percent of the situations in which we are uncomfortable and going into a negative emotion.

When a patient is angering us, we want to immediately shift the focus from "Look what this person is doing to me," to "Look what *I'm* doing to me with my own blown up thoughts." This person just happens to be here in my office and has responded in such a way that I am triggering myself with my own errors of thinking.

And that's a twenty-minute, quick summary.

Author: Thanks, Norm. That was great.

APPENDIX IV
WHAT REALLY HAPPENED AT AMERICA'S GOT TALENT

When I decided to audition for *AGT*, I did not tell Howard Stern, who was my patient and one of the judges on the show. I simply sent in an audition tape in September of 2012, and the next January *AGT* invited me to audition for the producers. Every contestant is told to prepare a ninety-second audition, which I performed in New York City in February. The producers sent me to another room to audition for the executive producers, and then I was sent to the holding room, where all the contestants wait around. They taped me doing some other things, like walking in at the beginning of the clip. They also wired me for sound and set up a discussion with one of the other contestants. This "spontaneous" discussion required three or four takes until the director had what he wanted.

In March 2013, I got word that I had been chosen to audition for the "celebrity judges" on April 9. I called Howard and informed him for the first time that I had been chosen to audition. Two days before the audition, I went into the City to tape all the interview segments they showed. While I was there, the executive producer of the show pulled me aside and told me that they knew of my relationship with Howard. Understandably, it raised serious conflict-of-interest issues and therefore I wouldn't be allowed to advance in the competition.

I said, "So, no matter how well I do, I'm not going to Vegas?"

He replied, "You're not going to Vegas. Do you still want to audition?"

I had anticipated this, so I was ready with a suggestion that Howard recuse himself and that the other judges decide my fate on the show. The producer agreed.

In the YouTube clip,* you'll see me pacing nervously and taking deep breaths before my audition. Why? Because the director told me to do those things, and they taped it. In fact, I was very excited, but not nervous.

The actual audition went very well. Howard's feigned surprise at seeing me was all set up ahead of time. I was told he would do that after I introduced myself. During my act, the audience of fourteen hundred people was laughing so much I had to stop a few times to wait for the laughter to die down. The judges (except Mel B) were all laughing as well.

Heidi Klum spoke first. She said she really enjoyed the act and wanted to see more. Then Mel B said, "I didn't get it. I didn't think it was funny."

I remember thinking, "It's a gastroenterologist with a talking colon. What don't you get about that?" Well, when she made that remark, the audience booed her roundly. Of course, the booing was cut out of what was shown on TV, along with two-thirds of my act. Howie Mandel told me that I already had a career and that this show wanted to find performers who've been "struggling in the trenches for fifteen or twenty years."

When it came time for the voting, Heidi voted yes, Howie Mandel voted no, and then he turned to Mel B and said, "Well, girl, it's up to you." At that moment, the audience started cheering and chanting "*Vegas! Vegas!*" I was sure from what she had said earlier that she would vote no. However, she turned around in her chair to check the audience reaction, and the cheering grew louder.

---

* https://www.youtube.com/watch?v=9nP7gpou9qs

When she turned back toward me, she had a big smile on her face, and I thought, "My God, she's going to vote me through!" Suddenly, the executive producer came running in from the side, waving his hands in a "stop" movement, clamped his hands over her microphone, and said something to her. She voted no.

On the YouTube video, you see Howie and Mel vote no and then Heidi Klum say "sorry" to me. They made it seem as if this was her vote, but actually she was commiserating with me after the others voted me down.

So the "reality" of reality TV is that it's the producers' desired reality, not what really happens. But no matter. I'm thrilled that I did it. I had a ton of fun, got to perform ventriloquism for eleven million people in prime time, and enjoyed being a mini-celebrity for fifteen minutes or so.

And I already had a good day job.

ACKNOWLEDGMENTS

ALTHOUGH MINE IS THE ONLY name on the cover, without the guidance, support, and care of the people below, this book would not have happened. To all of them, I am eternally grateful.

- Anjanette ("AJ") Harper, my editor, has skillfully and with both the highest professionalism and greatest kindness guided me through the creation of this book, from the first time we sat down to discuss the table of contents through the very last time I hit "SEND."
- I am deeply indebted to Michael Port, author of *Steal the Show*. I read a review of his book in a magic magazine (yes, we have those), bought *Steal the Show*, and within four paragraphs of the opening author's note I knew I'd found a kindred spirit— someone else who recognized all the performances in life. I located Michael online, became his student, and have benefitted immensely from his guidance, friendship, and faith in me.
- Michael and his wife Amy (who is the *real* show-stealer) founded Heroic Public Speaking and have become my invaluable mentors and friends. It is they who gave me the courage and tools to launch my post-practice speaking career and taught me the true meaning and power of *Yes, and*.
- Similarly, my Heroic Public Speaking family—and I do not use that word loosely—have encouraged my new life every step of the way. Particular thanks to Buck Adams, Mike Ganino, Jody Johnson, RN, Tony Mayo, Susan Sandler, Kim Shivler, and Drs. Arjun Rayapudi and Theo Tsaousides.

- Barry Friedman, retired four-time World Juggling Champion and one helluva business/creativity consultant, has been my coach, friend, and confidant. This is a guy who flew from California to New York just to watch me rehearse my keynote speech. His enthusiasm for this project and his belief in me have energized me the whole way.
- Writing coach Clementina Esposito helped me craft the keynote speech which is the basis of the book, and journalist Brenda Barbosa encapsulated my thoughts in one sentence that lit the proverbial fire under my proverbial *tuches.*
- Business author Mike Michalowicz generously shared the tools, tips, and techniques that he has accumulated while becoming a five-time best selling author. Heck, he even shared his knock-'em-dead margarita recipe.
- Buck Adams, Corinne Case, PA, Domenic Chiarella, David Crone, Mike Ganino, JoAnne Gottridge, MD, Steve Haar, Samuel Harrington, MD, Norman Kanter, PhD, Marilyn Klainberg, RN, PhD, Jody Johnson, RN, Joseph Masiuk, Esq., Scott Miller, Andy Nyman, Jack Rubenstein, MD, Scott Replogle, MD, Adam Smith, DO, and Ken Weber all kindly sat for interviews and contributed invaluable content.
- Kerrianne Cartmer-Edwards of Kickass Impact started as my branding expert and became my web guru, adviser, and friend. Her creativity, passion, enthusiasm, and tireless efforts have been a boost every step of the way. And what a fun lunch we had in Covent Garden!
- Choi Messer took my rather inchoate ideas and from them skillfully created the designs of both the cover and the text.
- Nicki Harper, copy editor, and Zoë Bird and Linda Morris, proofreaders, improved my writing and saved me from the eternal embarrassment of seeing spelling and punctuation errors appear in print.

- Danielle Libine's mastery of body language and photography somehow enabled her to take pictures that make me look so much better than I think I do.
- I am deeply grateful to the health professionals from medicine, nursing, social work, business, and psychology who took the time out of their busy lives to read the manuscript and offered invaluable feedback. Their suggestions have made this a better book: Steve Bedwell, MD, Clifford Berck, MD, Barry Cohen, MD, Michael Cohen, MD, Vincent deLuise, MD, Daniel Gensler, PhD, JoAnne Gottridge, MD, Samuel Harrington, MD, Matthew Horowitz, MD, Jody Johnson, RN, Charles Joseph, MD, Norman Kanter, PhD, Marilyn Klainberg, RN, PhD, Raj Madhok, MD, Mike Maione, Christina Park, MD, Scott Replogle, MD, Kedar Sankholkar, MD, Simeon Schwartz, MD, Adam Smith, DO, Richard Mark Steinbook, MD, and Page Valerie Tolbert, LCSW.
- JoAnne Gottridge, MD and Thomas McGinn, MD of the Department of Medicine of Northwell Health gave me my first opportunities to present the ideas in the book to other physicians.
- The late Carroll "Doc" Behrhorst and the Cakchiquel indigenous people, descendants of the Maya and patients at Clinica Behrhorst in Chilmaltenango, Guatemala, taught me as a medical student there on elective how to be a doctor with no more equipment than my stethoscope, my knowledge, and my heart.
- My medical practice partners, David Cohen, Michael Cohen, Barry Cohen (no, they're not related), Jay Kugler, Christina Park, Patrick Chang, and Matt Horowitz were my away-from-home family as well as friends and masters of the curbside consult. My secretary, Maria Deguglielmi, and my medical assistant and office wife, Gail Edwards, made my job easier every day.

- My children, Adam, Danielle, Ashley, Zoë, Charlotte, Dylan, and Hannah bring me joy most days, *tsuris* some days, and pride in the fine human beings they are every single day.
- Finally, and most important, my wife, Marcia Hecht, has supported and encouraged me in this project from inkling to completion. She inspired me when I was stuck or discouraged. She brought her English teacher's sense and sensibility along with her red pencil (actually, a pink pen) to my writing and thereby improved it immeasurably. And, most of all, she has loved me even better than she did when we were teenagers.

ABOUT THE AUTHOR

BOB BAKER, MD IS AN internist/gastroenterologist who left private practice after 35 years in a multi-specialty group in Great Neck, New York. He has a special interest in the doctor-patient relationship and served as a Physician Master Facilitator for the Culture of C.A.R.E. program of Northwell Health, one of the country's largest health systems.

Dr. Baker is a graduate of Princeton University and the College of Physicians and Surgeons of Columbia University. He trained at New York Hospital/Cornell Medical Center and completed his fellowship in gastroenterology at Beth Israel Hospital/Harvard Medical School.

He is also a professional magician and ventriloquist who has appeared on *America's Got Talent* as well at as numerous private, corporate, and fundraising events. His performing skills play an important role in making him a highly-praised, in-demand keynote speaker for doctors, nurses, and other healthcare workers at medical conferences and meetings.

Dr. Baker lives on Long Island with his wife and whichever of his seven children happen to be around.

REFERENCES

Introduction

[1] Shakespeare, William. *As You Like It, Act II, Scene VII.*

Chapter 1: Our Changing Medical World

[1] "Doctor Tops List of Prestigious Occupations," The Harris Poll, posted March 29, 2006, http://www.theharrispoll.com/business/Doctor-Tops-List-Prestigious-Occupations.html.

[2] The Future of Healthcare. A National Survey of Physicians. The Doctors Company. February 29, 2012.

[3] Anonymous, "What Doctors Want Their Patients to Know," *Consumer Reports,* March, 2011, 20.

[4] Daniela Drake, "How Being a Doctor Became the Most Miserable Profession," *The Daily Beast,* April 14, 2014.

[5] Sandeep Jauhar, *DOCTORED The Disillusionment of an American Physician* (New York: Farrar, Straus and Giroux, 2014).

[6] Gaby Loria, "How Patients Use Online Reviews," accessed December 18, 2017, https://www.softwareadvice.com/resources/how-patients-use-online-reviews.

[7] Vanguard Communications, "Vanguard Analysis Finds Online Doctor Reviews Overwhelmingly Positive," accessed December 18, 2017, https://vanguardcommunications.net/analysis-finds-online-doctor-reviews-positive.

[8] Niam Yaraghi, "Online Medical Reviews of Providers: Take Them with a Grain of Salt," accessed March 1, 2017, https://www.brookings.edu/blog/techtank/2015/06/16/online-reviews-of-medical-providers-take-them-with-a-grain-of-salt.

[9] S. Wang, "What Doctors Are Doing About Bad Reviews Online," *Wall Street Journal,* June 26, 2017.

[10] Quoted in Bruce Japsen, "Ouch! Patient Satisfaction Hits Physician Pay," *Forbes*, July 2, 2013.

[11] Matthew P. Manary, MS, William Boulding, PhD, Richard Staelin, PhD, and Seth W. Glickman, MD, MBA, "The Patient Experience and Health Outcomes," *New England Journal of Medicine* 368 (2013): 201-203.

[12] A. Zgierska, D. Rabago, and M.M. Miller, "Impact of Patient Satisfaction Ratings on Physicians and Clinical Care," *Patient Preference and Adherence* 8 (2014): 437–446.

[13] Amednewscom, "Incentive Pay Prevalence Echoes Boom in Employed Physicians. Employers Are Shifting toward Quality of Care and Away from the Number of Patients Physicians See," accessed June 30, 2017, *American Medical New*, posted January 2, 2013.

CHAPTER 2: THE PATIENT VISIT IS A PERFORMANCE

[1] Erving Goffman, *The Presentation of Self in Everyday Life* (New York: Anchor Books, 1959), p. 15.

[2] Michael Port, *Steal the Show: From Speeches to Job Interviews to Deal-Closing Pitches, How to Guarantee a Standing Ovation for All the Performances in Your Life*. (Houghton Mifflin Harcourt, 2015).

[3] Marcus Geduld, "Acting: What makes a compelling performance?" accessed April 20, 2017, *Quora.com*, September 29, 2013.

[4] Shakespeare, William. *As You Like It. Act II, Scene VII*.

[5] Erving Goffman, *The Presentation of Self in Everyday Life* (New York: Anchor Books, 1959).

[6] James Merlino, *Service Fanatics: How to Build Superior Patient Experience the Cleveland Clinic Way* (New York: McGraw Hill Education, 2015).

[7] S.M. Sanbonmatsu, D.L. Strayer, N. Medeiros-Ward, and J.M. Watson, "Who Multi-Tasks and Why? Multi-Tasking Ability, Perceived Multi-Tasking Ability, Impulsivity, and Sensation Seeking," *PLOS One* 8, no. 1 (2013), https://doi.org/10.1371/journal.pone.0054402.

[8] D.L. Strayer, F.A. Drews, and D.J. Crouch, "A Comparison of the Cell Phone Driver and the Drunk Driver," *Human Factors* 48, no. 2 (Summer 2006): 381-91.

[9] Theo Tsaousides, *Brain Blocks*. (New York: Prentice Hall Press, 2015), p. 100.

[10] M. Iacoboni, Mirroring People. *The Science of Empathy and How We Connect with Others*. (New York: Farrar, Strauss and Giroux, 2008).

[11] R.I.M. Dunbar, K. Kaskatis, I. MacDonald, and V. Barra, "Performance of Music Elevates Pain Threshold and Positive Affect: Implications for the Evolutionary Function of Music," *Evolutionary Psychology* 10, no. 4, (October 1, 2012).

CHAPTER 3: *I'm Not a Performer and Don't Want to Be*

[1] "Value of the Liberal Arts in a Pre-medical Education," Missouri State University, accessed May 23, 2017, http://www.missouristate.edu/bms/CMB/LiberalArts.htm.

[2] "The Value of a Liberal Arts Education," My Wellesley, Mission and Values, accessed December 18, 2017, http://www.wellesley.edu/about/missionandvalues/valueliberalarts#XSI8sTtdcOY7Mpr2.97.

[3] *The Disney Look.* "Good Judgment and Stage Presence," p. 3. Accessed January 28, 2018, http://cdn.disneycareers.com/managed/DisneyLookBook3_7_FINAL.pdf.

CHAPTER 4: *What Patients Want*

[1] "Top Complaints Posted on Doc-Rating Websites," Medscape, Feb 20, 2014, https://www.medscape.com/viewarticle/820809.

[2] D.R. Rhoades, K.F. McFarland, W.H. Finch, and A.O. Johnson, "Speaking and Interruptions during Primary Care Office Visits," *Family Medicine* 33, no. 7 (2001): 528-32.

[3] Osler, William, *The Principles and Practice of Medicine*, 1892.

[4] Medscape, *op. cit.*

[5] Osler, *op. cit.*

[6] Merlino, *op. cit.* p.125.

[7] M. Tai-Seale, T.G. McGuire, and W. Zhang, "Time Allocation in Primary Care Office Visits," *Health Services Research* 42, no. 5 (Oct 2007): 1871-1894.

[8] Merlino, *op. cit.* p. 126.

CHAPTER 5: *The Five Basic Performance Techniques We Need*

[1] For the sake of accuracy, here's what Hoffman told interviewer Neil Conan on NPR's *Talk of the Nation* on December 4, 2003: Well, it's—you know, it's become, God knows, more than slightly distorted. I told that story to *Time*

magazine and then they reinterpreted it because it made a better story. I was in New York shooting. My marriage, first marriage, was falling apart. It was a good excuse to party. And, you know, the reason to stay up for two days wasn't just because the character stayed up two days. It was because, you know, I was partying, it was Studio 54. And I rationalized it by saying, you know—so that was, I think, the deeper reason.

When I got to Los Angeles and we continued filming and I was laughing, you know, talking to—I called him Lordage—talking to Lordage about this. We both laughed and he said—he says, 'Why don't you try acting?' But there was irony there, which I said in the *Time* interview, which unfortunately was left out.

[2] Constantin Stanislavski, *An Actor Prepares* (New York: Routledge, 1955), pp. 177-208.

[3] Quoted in Robert Faires, "Acting is Listening," *The Austin Chronicle*, Nov. 12, 2010.

[4] Quoted in John Walcott, "The Power of Listening and Reacting: Actors Listen Up!" accessed June 5, 2017, http://tophollywoodactingcoach.com/2014/04/listening-and-reacting-are-power-on-camera.

[5] A. Mehrabian, *Nonverbal communication* (Aldine-Atherton, Chicago, Illinois, 1972).

[6] Michael Argyle, *Bodily Communication* (New York: Rutledge, 2010).

[7] A. Trimboli, and M. Walker, "Nonverbal Dominance in the Communication of Affect: A Myth?" Journal of Nonverbal Behavior 11, no. 3 (1987): 180-190.

[8] D. Matsumoto, and H.S. Hwang, "Reading Facial Expressions of Emotion," *American Psychological Association Science Briefs*, May 2011, http://www.apa.org/science/about/psa/2011/05/facial-expressions.aspx.

[9] I have no relationship, financial or otherwise, with the organization promoting this test and course.

[10] See the discussion of Empathetics in Chapter 12, What Others Say.

[11] Bodhipaksa, "Being 'in the moment'," posted February 16, 2007. http://www.wildmind.org/background/moment.

[12] Westbrook, Mark, "Being in the Moment Just Sounds Pretty Wanky to Me," accessed June 20, 2017, https://actingcoachscotland.co.uk/blog/being-moment-just-sounds-pretty-wanky-me/.

[13] M.A. Killingsworth, and D.T. Gilbert, "A Wandering Mind is an Unhappy Mind," *Science* Nov. 12, 2010, p. 932.

[14] Matt Killingsworth, "Want to Be Happier? Stay in the Moment," Filmed November, 2011 at TEDxCambridge, Video, 10:16, https://www.ted.com/talks/matt_killingsworth_want_to_be_happier_stay_in_the_moment.

[15] Anonymous, "Where Have You Gone, Joe DiMaggio?" The Sporting News (April 4, 1951). P.S.

[16] Erving, Goffman, The Presentation of Self in Everyday Life (New York: Anchor Books, 1959).

[17] ibid., pp. 17-19.

[18] Charles Northrup, "Staying in Character When Other Actors Are Speaking," accessed December 18, 2017, http://northrup.tripod.com/staying.html.

[19] Ruth Kulerman, "Keeping in Character," Actor Tip, accessed December 18, 2017, https://actortips.com/keeping-in-character/https://actortips.com/keeping-in-character/.

[20] Alex Korb, "Smile: A Powerful Tool," Psychology Today blog. August 1, 2012, https://www.psychologytoday.com/blog/prefrontal-nudity/201208/smile-powerful-tool.

[21] C. Wilkes, R. Kidd, M. Sagar, and E. Broadbent, "Upright Posture Improves Affect and Fatigue in People with Depressive Symptoms," Journal of Behavioral Therapy and Experimental Psychology 54 (March 2017): 143–149.

[22] Amy Cuddy, "Your Body Language May Shape Who You Are," Filmed June, 2012 at TEDGlobal 2012. 19:15, https://ted.com/talks/amy_cuddy_your_body_language_shapes_who_you_are/.

[23] R. Pascale, J. Sternin and M. Sternin, The Power of Positive Deviance: How Unlikely Innovators Solve the World's Toughest Problems E-book. Boston: Harvard Business School Publishing, 2010, Kindle Edition.

[24] M.I. Slepian, K.R. Bogart and N. Ambady, "Thin-slice Judgments in the Clinical Context" Rev. Clin. Psychol. 10 (2014): 131-53.

[25] M. Gladwell, Blink: The Power of Thinking Without Thinking (Boston: Back Bay Books, 2007).

CHAPTER 6: SETTING THE STAGE: WHAT TO DO BEFORE YOU GO IN WITH THE PATIENT

[1] Mike Abramson, When Does the Show Begin? accessed June 30, 2017, https://www.stagerights.com/blog/when-does-show-begin/.

[2] Vanguard Communications, "Online Complaints? Blame Customer Service, Not Doctors' Care," accessed December 18, 2017, https://vanguardcommunications.net/patient-complaints.

[3] An excellent book on physician office décor by Ann Sloan Devlin: *Transforming the Doctor's Office* (Philadelphia: Routledge, 2014).

[4] Sam Gosling, *Snoop. What Your Stuff Says About You* (New York: Basic Books, 2008).

[5] Danielle Ofri, "In a Culture of Disrespect, Patients Lose Out," *New York Times*, July 18, 2013.

[6] David Maister, "The Psychology of Waiting Lines," posted 1985, accessed June 18, 2017, http://davidmaister.com/articles/the-psychology-of-waiting-lines/.

[7] D. Kahneman, "Evaluation by Moments: Past and Future," In D. Kahneman and A. Tversky (Eds.) *Choices, Values and Frames.* (New York: Cambridge University Press, 2000) chapter 38, pp. 693-708.

[8] R. Youngson, *Time to Care: How to Love Your Patients and Your Job* (Ragland, New Zealand: Rebelheart Publishers, 201), p. 132.

[9] Merlino, *op. cit.* p. 127.

[10] A. Durayappah-Harrison, "What Science Has to Say About Genuine vs. Fake Smiles," *Psychology Today* online, posted January 5, 2010.

[11] Mark Bowden, *Tame the Primitive Brain* (New York: John Wiley & Sons. 2013, e-book).

CHAPTER 7: IN THE ROOM WITH THE PATIENT

[1] M. Lavin, "What Doctors Should Call Their Patients," *Journal of Medical Ethics* 14, no. 3 (1988): 129-31 is a good place to start.

R.C. Senelick, "What's In a Name: What Should Patients and Doctors Call Each Other?" *Huffington Post*, March 19, 2014 is also a good beginning.

[2] K.J. Swayden, K.K. Anderson, L.M. Connelly, *et al.*, "Effect of Sitting vs. Standing on Perception of Provider Time at Bedside: A Pilot Study," *Patient Education and Counseling* 86, no. 2 (2012): 166-71.

[3] N. Ambady, D. LaPlante, T. Nguyen, *et al.* "Surgeons' Tone of Voice: A Clue to Malpractice History," *Surgery* 132 (2002): pp. 5-9.

[4] J. Hecht, "Is the Gaze from Those Big Puppy Eyes the Look of Your Doggie's Love?" *Scientific American* online, April 16, 2015.

[5] B. Auyeung, M.V. Lombardo, M. Heinrichs, *et al.* "Oxytocin Increases Eye Contact during a Real-time, Naturalistic Social Interaction in Males with

and without Autism," *Translational Psychiatry* 5, e507; doi:10.1038/tp. 2014.146, published online February 10, 2015.

[6] D.R. Rhoades, K.F. McFarland, W.H. Finch and A.O. Johnson, "Speaking and Interruptions during Primary Care Office Visits," *Family Medicine* 33, no. 7 (2001): 528-32.

[7] H.B. Beckman, and R.M. Frankel, "The Effect of Physician Behavior on the Collection of Data," *Annals of Internal Medicine* 101, no. 5 (1984): 692-6.

[8] L. Marcinowicz, J. Konstantynowicz, and C. Godlweski, "Patients' Perceptions of GP Non-verbal Communication: A Qualitative Study," *British Journal of General Practice* 60, no. 571 (2010): 83-87.

[9] R.S. Margalit, D. Roter, M.A. and Dunevant, *et al.*, "Electronic Medical Record Use and Physician-patient Communication: An Observational Study of Israeli Primary Care Encounters," *Patient Education and Counseling* 61, no. 1 (2006): 134-41.

[10] C. Heath, "Participation in the Medical Consultation: The Co-ordination of Verbal and Nonverbal Behavior between the Doctor and the Patient," *Sociology of Health & Illness*, 6, no. 3 (1984): 311-88.

CHAPTER 8: THE PERFORMANCE MUST GO ON

[1] Jan Hoffman, "The Anxiety of Waiting for Test Results," *New York Times.* July 23, 2012.

[2] R. Ruiz-Moral, L.A. Perula de Torres, and I. Jaramillo-Martin, "The Effect of Patients' Met Expectations on Consultation Outcomes. A Study with Family Medicine Residents," *Journal of General Internal Medicine* 22, no. 1 (2007): 86–91.

[3] A. Bowling, G. Rowe, and M. McKee, "Patients' Experiences of Their Healthcare in Relation to Their Expectations and Satisfaction: A Population Survey," *Journal of the Royal Society of Medicine* 106, no. 4 (2013): 143-9.

[4] Youngson, *op. cit.* p. 30.

[5] Brooke Billingsley, *The Perceptive Patient: A Healthcare Consultant's Own Cancer Journey* (Indianapolis: Perceptive Strategies, 2016).

[6] Eric Goldman, "How Doctors Should Respond to Negative Online Reviews," *Forbes*, Nov. 21, 2013.

[7] Jay Baer, *Hug Your Haters* (New York: Portfolio/Penguin, 2016).

CHAPTER 9: MORE TECHNIQUES TO TRY: IMPROVISATION AND STORYTELLING

[1] M. Leon, "Medically Relevant Improv: Using Improvisation to Teach Empathic Communication to Medical Professionals," Accessed September 5, 2017. http://scholarship.rollins.edu/honors/13.

[2] V. Giang, "Why Top Companies and MBA Programs are Teaching Improv," *Fast Company,* January 13, 3016.

[3] K. Watson, "Perspective: Serious Play: Teaching Medical Skills with Improvisational Theater Techniques," *Academic Medicine* 86 no. 10 (2011): 1260-65.

[4] M. Besser, I. Roberts, and M. Walsh, *The Upright Citizens Brigade Comedy Improvisation Manual.* New York: Comedy Council of Nicea, LLC, 2013, p.12.

[5] Schwartz, Tony. "The Power of Starting with 'Yes'. *New York Times,* April 17, 2015.

[6] B. Boynton, *Medical Improv: A New Way to Improve Communication.* (Seattle: CreateSpace, 2017).

T. Goldstein and E. Winner, "Enhancing Empathy and Theory of Mind," *Journal of Cognition and Development* 13, no. 1 (2012): 19-37.

[7] Uri Hasson. *This Is Your Brain on Communication,* Filmed February, 2016 at TED 2016, video, 2:57, https://ted.com/talks/uri_hasson_this_is_your_brain_on_communication.

[8] Bruce Jones. "Leadership Lessons From Walt Disney: The Power of Storytelling, *Talking Point: The Disney Institute Blog,* Nov. 4, 2014.

CHAPTER 10: PUTTING IT ALL TO WORK

[1] P. Lally, C. vanJaarsveld, H.W.W. Potts, and J. Wardle, "How Are Habits Formed: Modeling Habit Formation in the Real World," *European Journal of Social Psychology* 40, no. 6 (2010): 998-1009.

[2] Kory Grow, "Paul McCartney Talks One on One Tour, Pre-Stage Rituals, Rap as Poetry, *Rolling Stone* July 10, 2017.

CHAPTER 11: WHEN THINGS GO WRONG

[1] David H. Nathan, *The McFarland Baseball Quotations Dictionary.* (Jefferson, NC: McFarland & Company, 2000).

[2] R.R. Peto, L.M. Tenerowicz, E.M. Benjamin, *et al.*, "One System's Journey in Creating a Disclosure and Apology Program," *Joint Commission Journal on Quality and Patient Safety* 35, no. 10 (2009): 487-96.

[3] A. Kachalia, S.R. Kaufman, MA; R. Richard Boothman, *et al.*, "Liability Claims and Costs Before and After Implementation of a Medical Error Disclosure Program," *Annals of internal medicine* 153, no. 4 (August 2010): 213.

[4] L. Leape, Institute of Healthcare Improvement Open School, Accessed June 28, 2017, http://www.ihi.org/education/IHIOpenSchool/resources/Pages/Activities/ApologizingEffectivelytoPatientsandFamilies.aspx.

[5] Massachusetts Coalition for the Prevention of Medical Errors, "When Things Go Wrong: Responding to Adverse Events," A consensus statement of the Harvard Hospitals March, 2006. http://www.macoalition.org/documents/respondingToAdverseEvents.pdf.

CHAPTER 12: WHAT OTHERS SAY

[1] Alan Alda, *If I Understood You, Would I Have This Look on My Face? My Adventures in the Art and Science of Relating and Communicating* (New York: Random House, 2017).

[2] Michael Port, *op. cit.*

[3] Youngson, *op. cit.* p. 114

[4] *Idem*, p. 133.

[5] *Idem*, p. 33.

[6] Scott Louis Diering, *Love Your Patients! Improving Patient Satisfaction with Essential Behaviors That Enrich the Lives of Patients & Professionals* (Nevada City, CA: Blue Dolphin Publishing, 2004).

[7] Thomas H. Lee, *An Epidemic of Empathy in Healthcare: How to Deliver Compassionate, Connected Patient Care That Creates a Competitive Advantage* (New York: McGraw Hill Education, 2016).

[8] Jacquelyn Small and Jim Mulry, *Improving Your Bedside Manner: A Handbook for Physicians to Develop Therapeutic Conversations with Their Patients* (Austin: Eupsychian Press, 2008).

[9] Merlino, *op. cit.*

[10] Stephen C. Beeson, *Practicing Excellence: A Physician's Manual to Exceptional Health Care* (Gulf Breeze, FL: Fire Starter Publishing, 2006).

CHAPTER 13: CURTAIN

[1] R.I. Dunbar, K. Kaskatis, I. MacDonald, and V. Barra, "Performance of Music Elevates Pain Threshold and Positive Affect: Implications for the Evolutionary Function of Music," *Evolutionary Psychology* 10, no. 4 (October, 2012): 688-702.

DOCTORS' STORY BANK IDEAS